DO YOU KNOW

Toads?

Written by
Alain M. Bergeron
Michel Quintin
Sampar

Illustrations by
Sampar

Translated by
Solange Messier

Fitzhenry & Whiteside

First published as "Savais-tu? Les Crapauds" by Éditions Michel Quintin, Québec, Canada

Published in Canada by Fitzhenry & Whiteside, 195 Allstate Parkway, Markham, Ontario L3R 4T8

Published in the United States by Fitzhenry & Whiteside, 311 Washington Street, Brighton, Massachusetts 02135

www.fitzhenry.ca godwit@fitzhenry.ca

10 9 8 7 6 5 4 3 2 1

Library and Archives Canada Cataloguing in Publication
Do You Know Toads?
ISBN 9781554553020 (pbk.)
Data available on file

Publisher Cataloging-in-Publication Data (U.S.)
Do You Know Toads?
ISBN 9781554553020 (pbk.)
Data available on file

Fitzhenry & Whiteside acknowledges with thanks the Canada Council for the Arts, and the Ontario Arts Council for their support of our publishing program. We acknowledge the financial support of the Government of Canada through the Canada Book Fund (CBF) for our publishing activities.

Canada Council for the Arts   Conseil des Arts du Canada

ONTARIO ARTS COUNCIL
CONSEIL DES ARTS DE L'ONTARIO
50 YEARS OF ONTARIO GOVERNMENT SUPPORT OF THE ARTS
50 ANS DE SOUTIEN DU GOUVERNEMENT DE L'ONTARIO AUX ARTS

Text and cover design by Daniel Choi
Cover image by Sampar
Printed in Canada by Friesens.

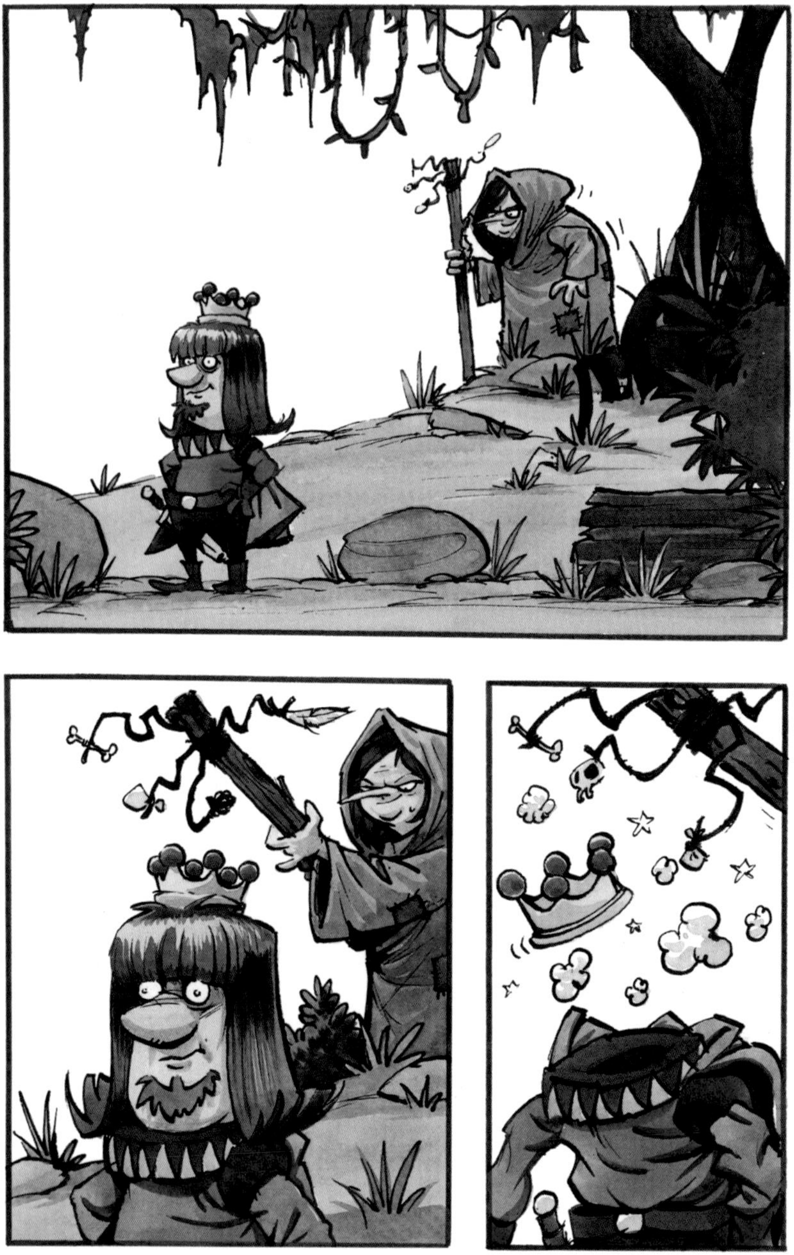

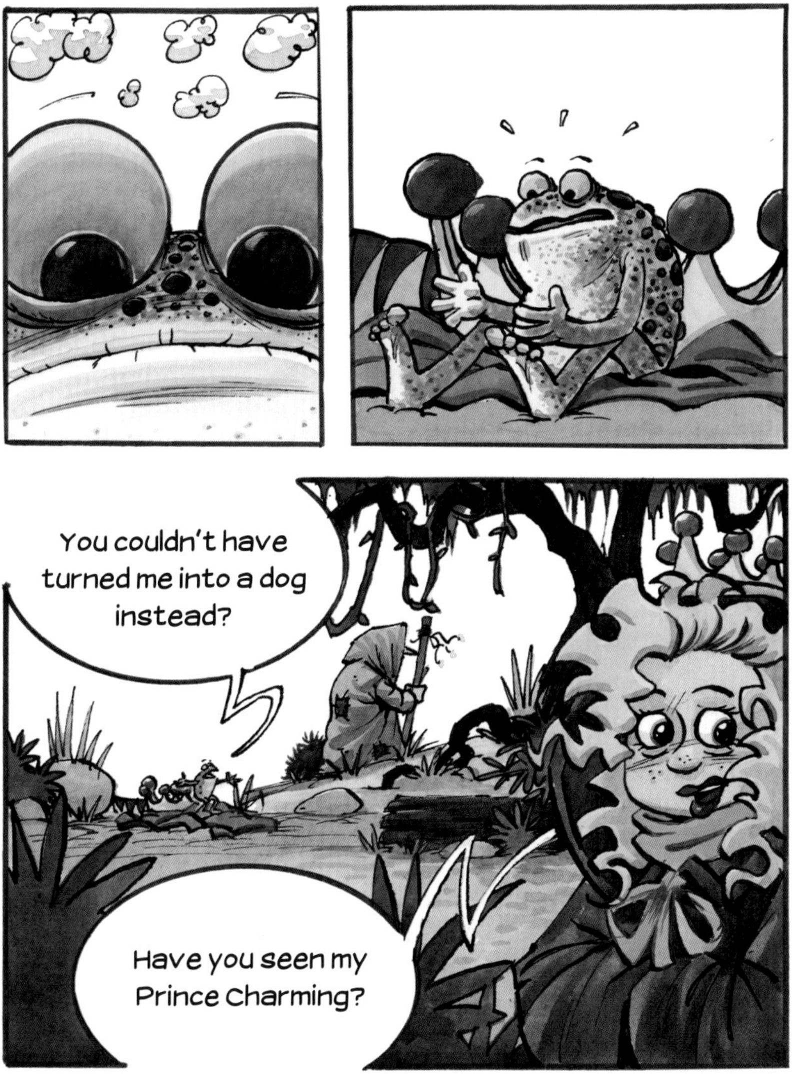
You couldn't have turned me into a dog instead?
Have you seen my Prince Charming?

Certain **species** are called toads even if they don't actually qualify as such. These species don't have the same physical characteristics that true toads have, like dry and warty skin.

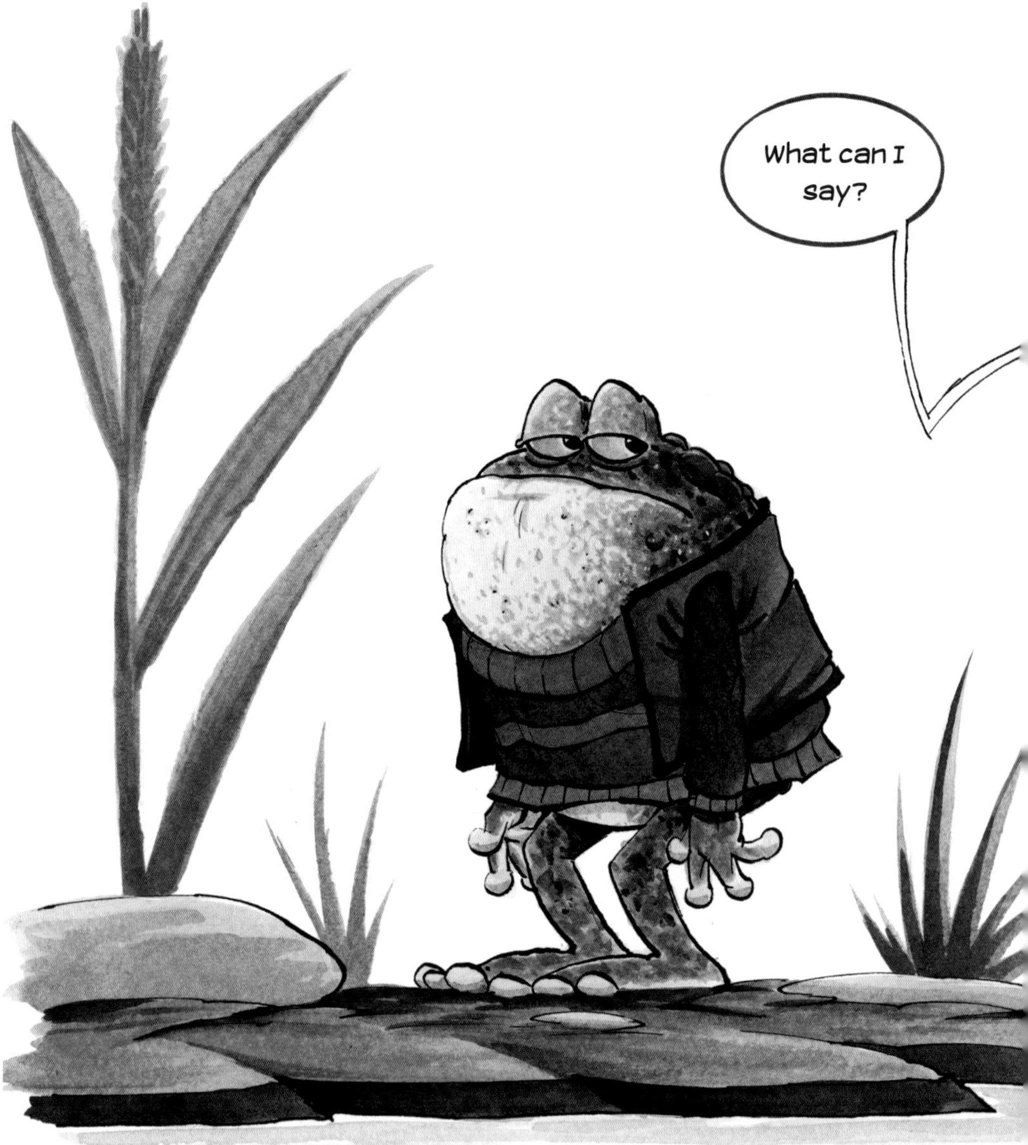
What can I say?

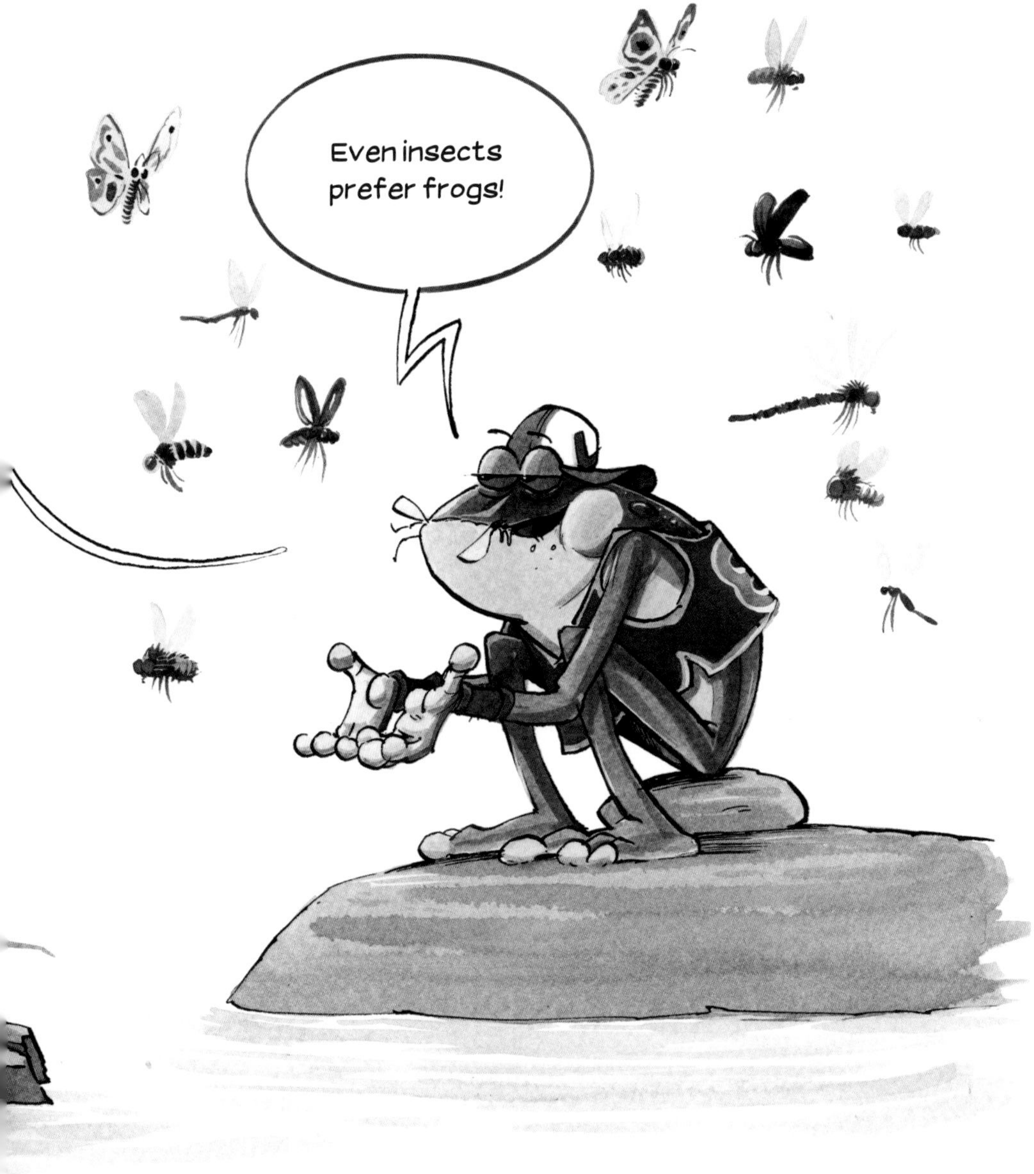
Even insects
prefer frogs!

Together, toads and frogs make up a group of 2,800 different species. Of these, barely 300 species are actual toads.

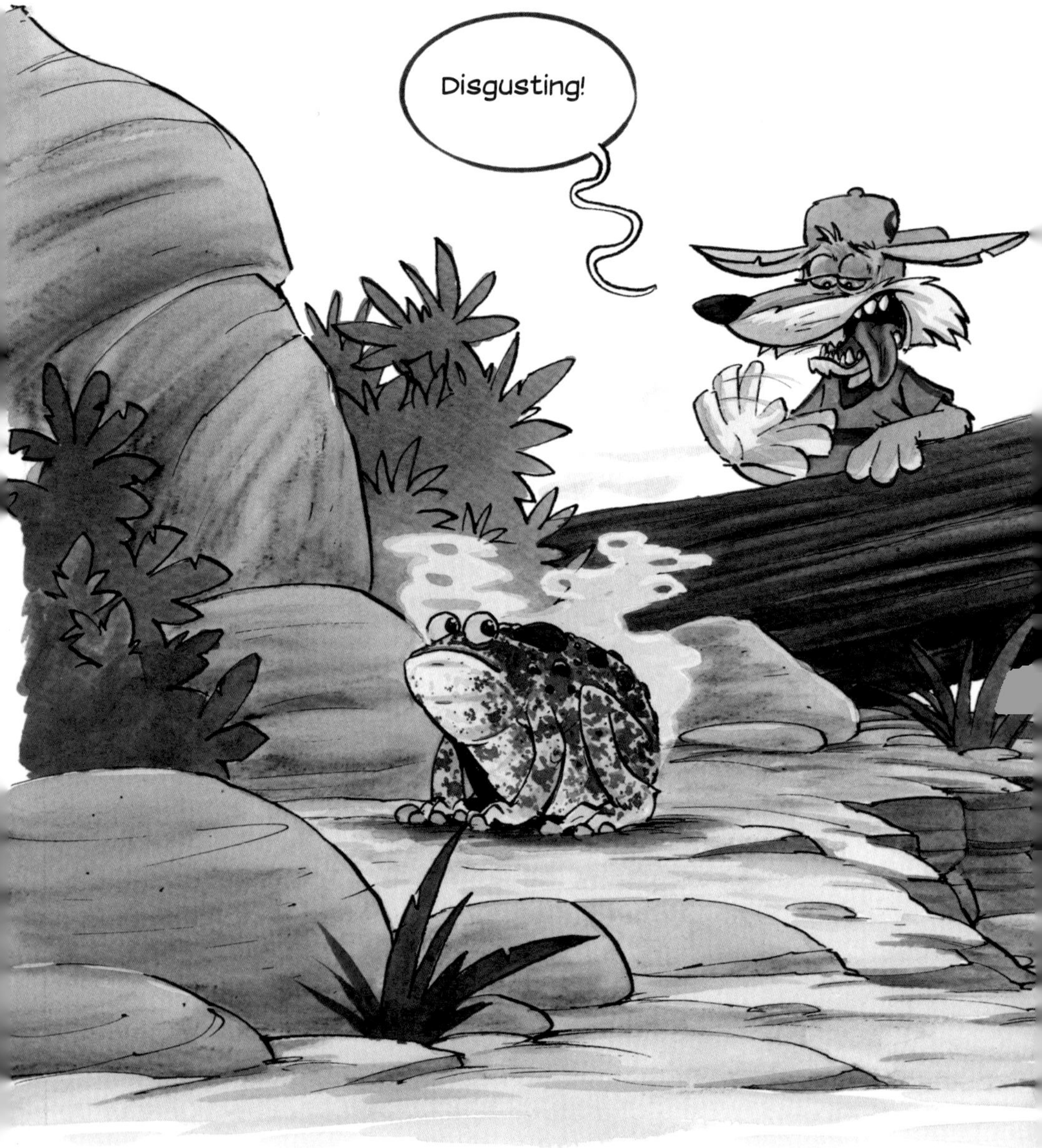
Disgusting!

Toad warts are made up of glands. These glands secrete a foul, bad-tasting poison that repels predators.

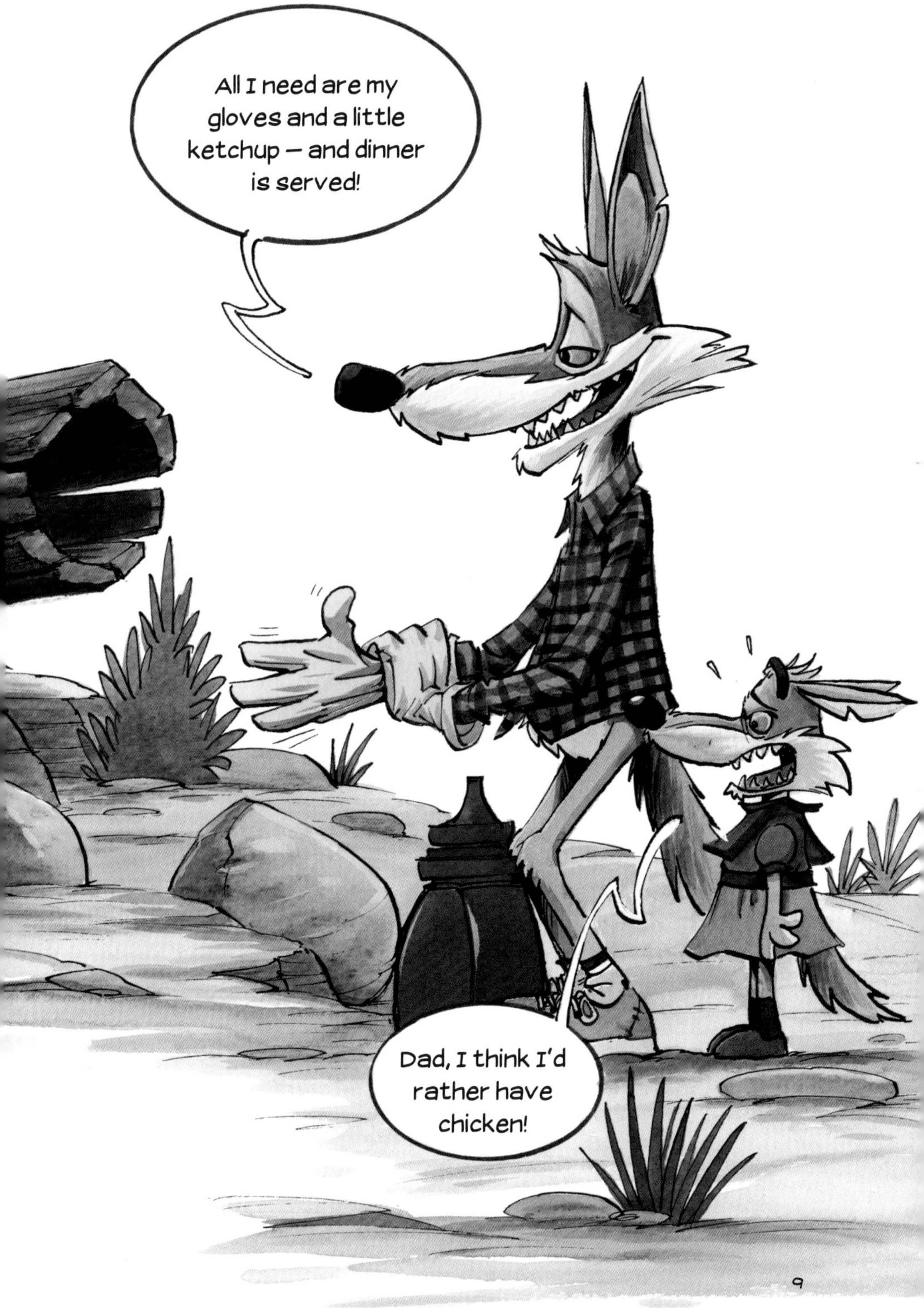
All I need are my gloves and a little ketchup – and dinner is served!
Dad, I think I'd rather have chicken!

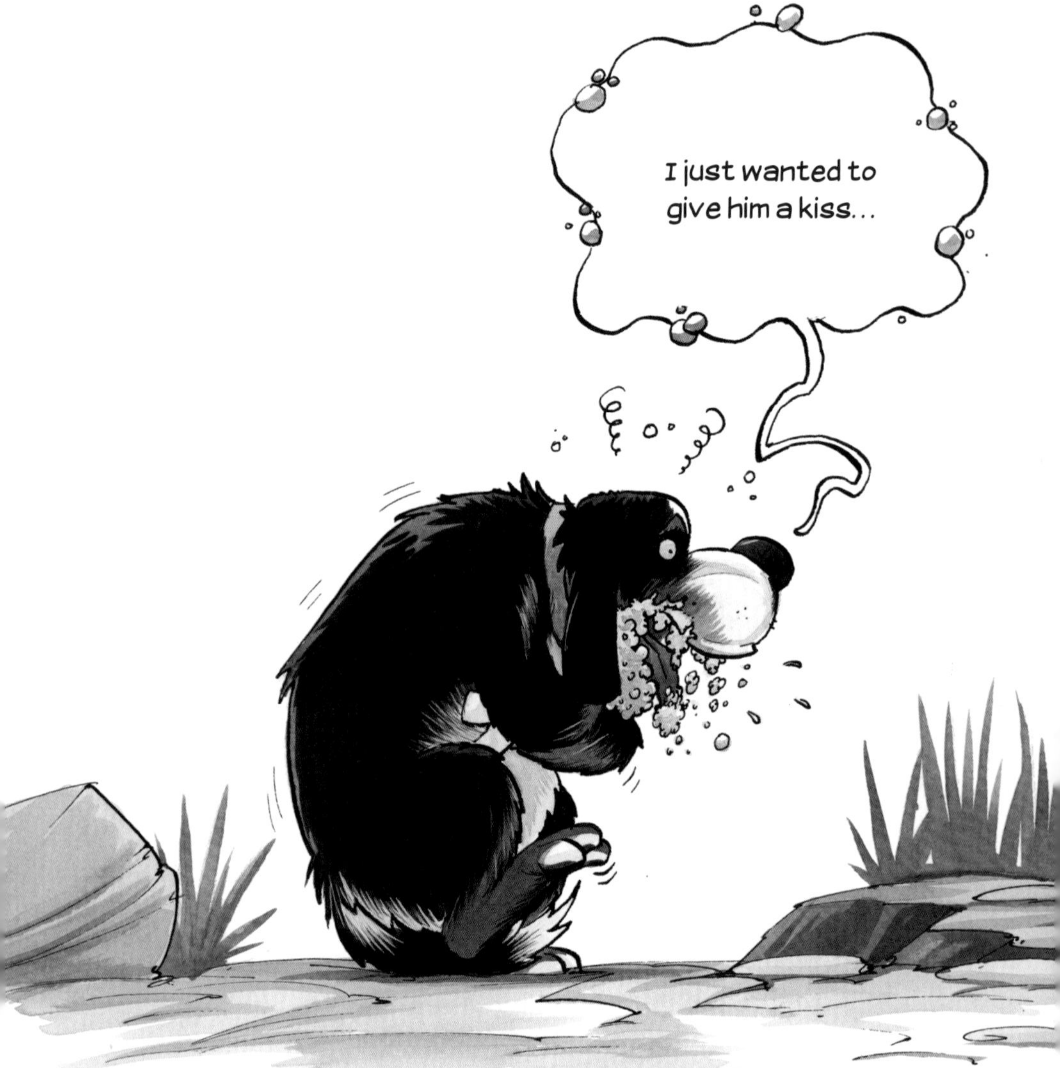
I just wanted to give him a kiss...

The poison secreted from certain species can sicken or even kill a snake or dog. Some people have even died from eating marine toads.

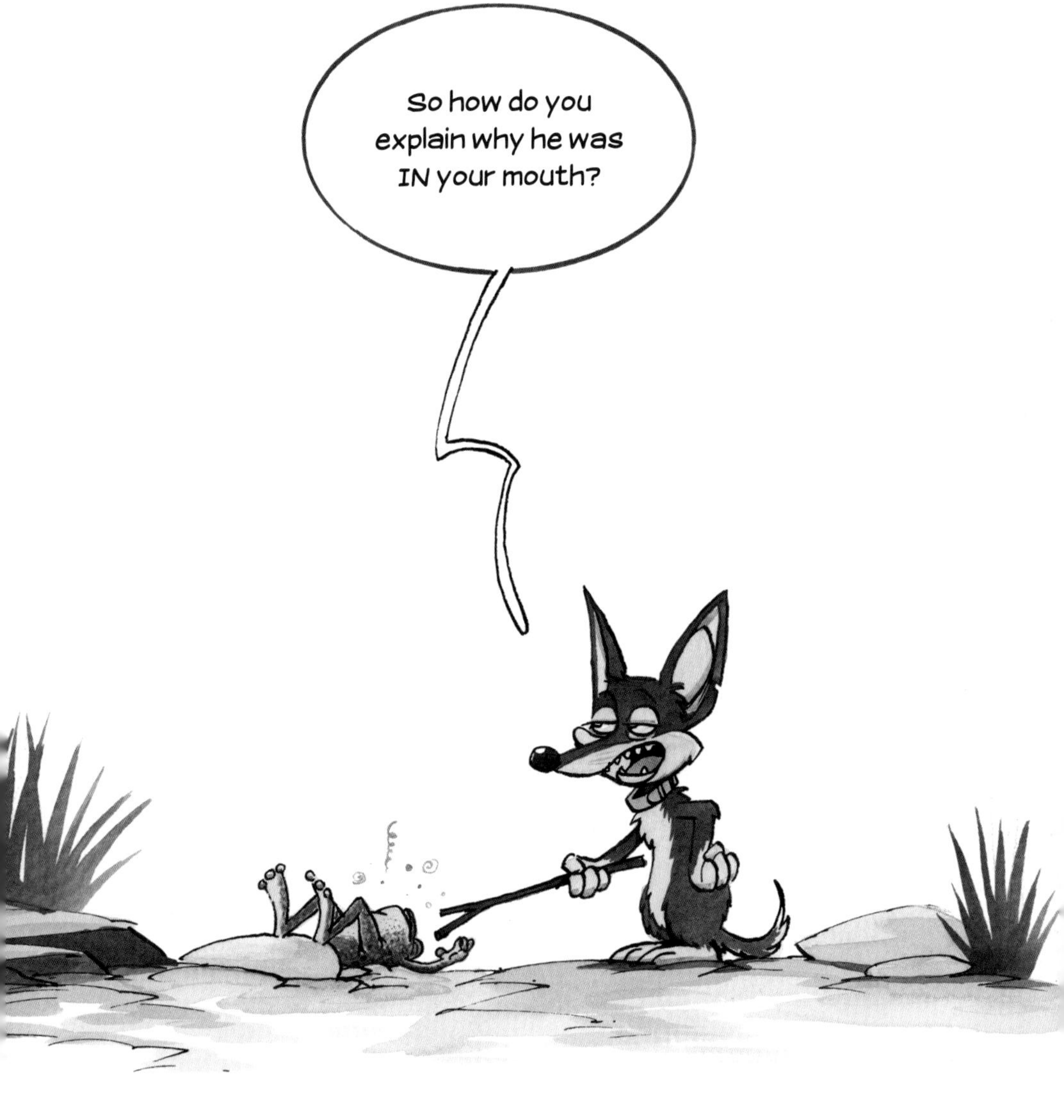
So how do you explain why he was IN your mouth?

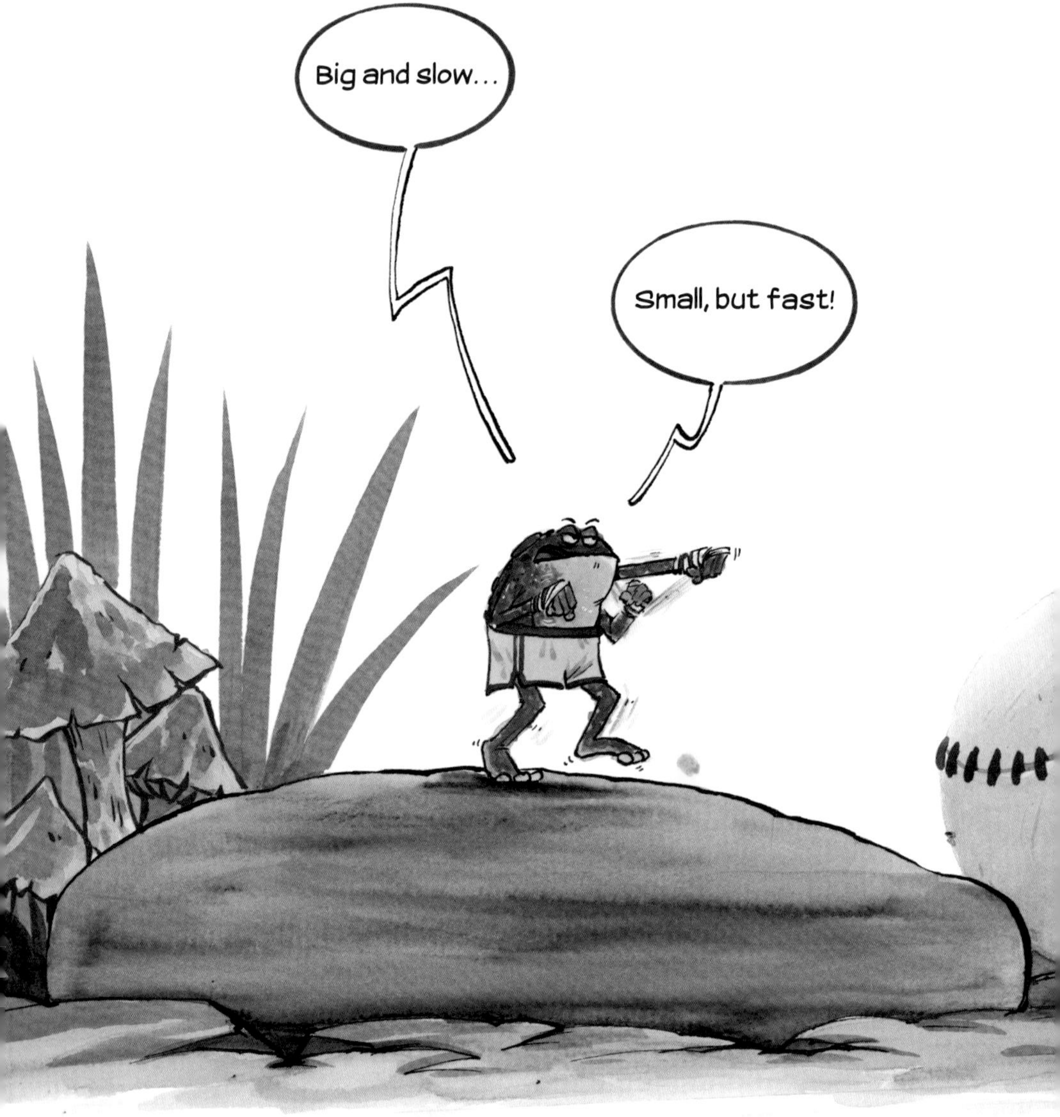
Big and slow...
Small, but fast!

The marine toad is the biggest of all toad species. It can reach 23 centimetres (9 in) in length.

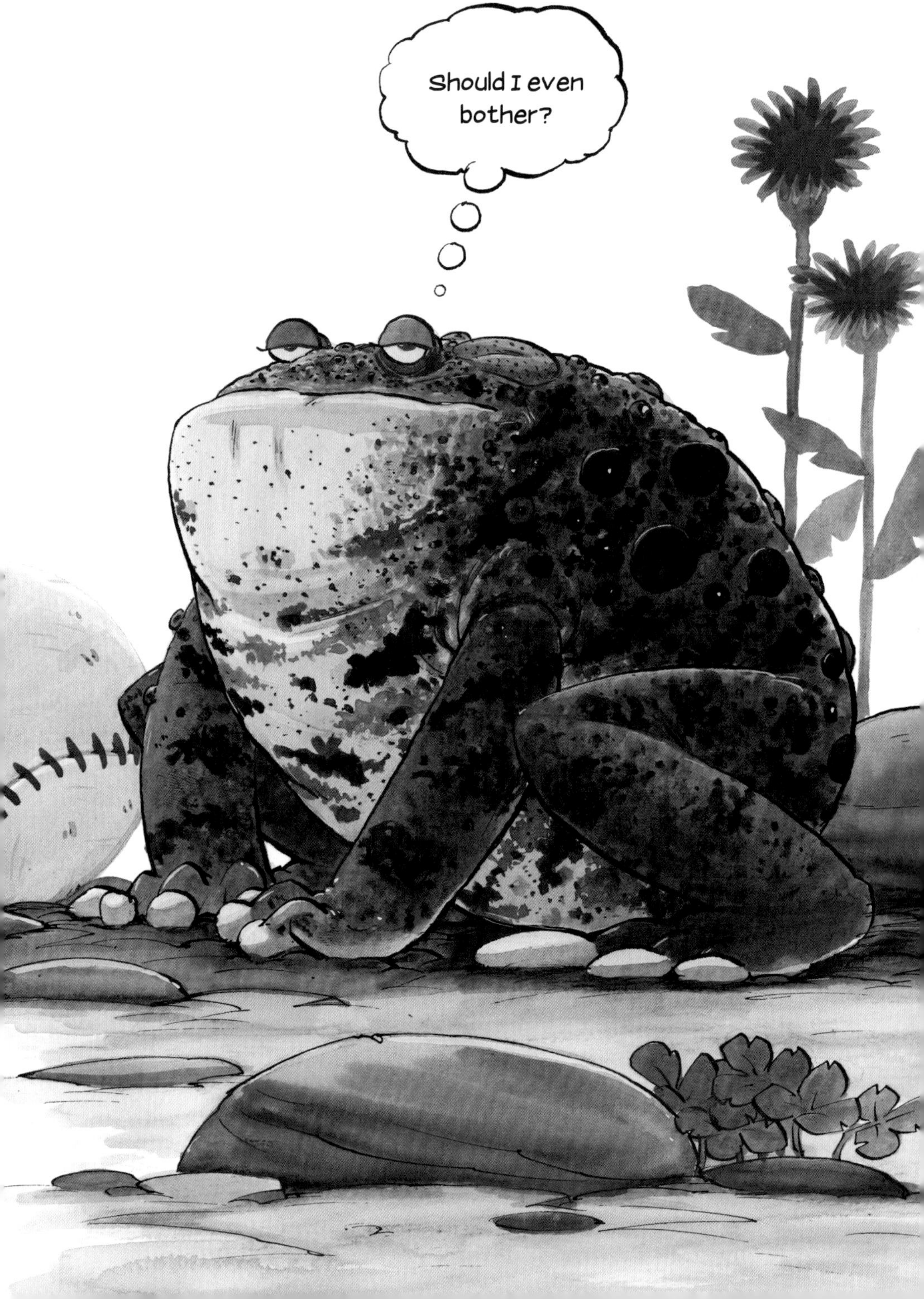
Should I even bother?

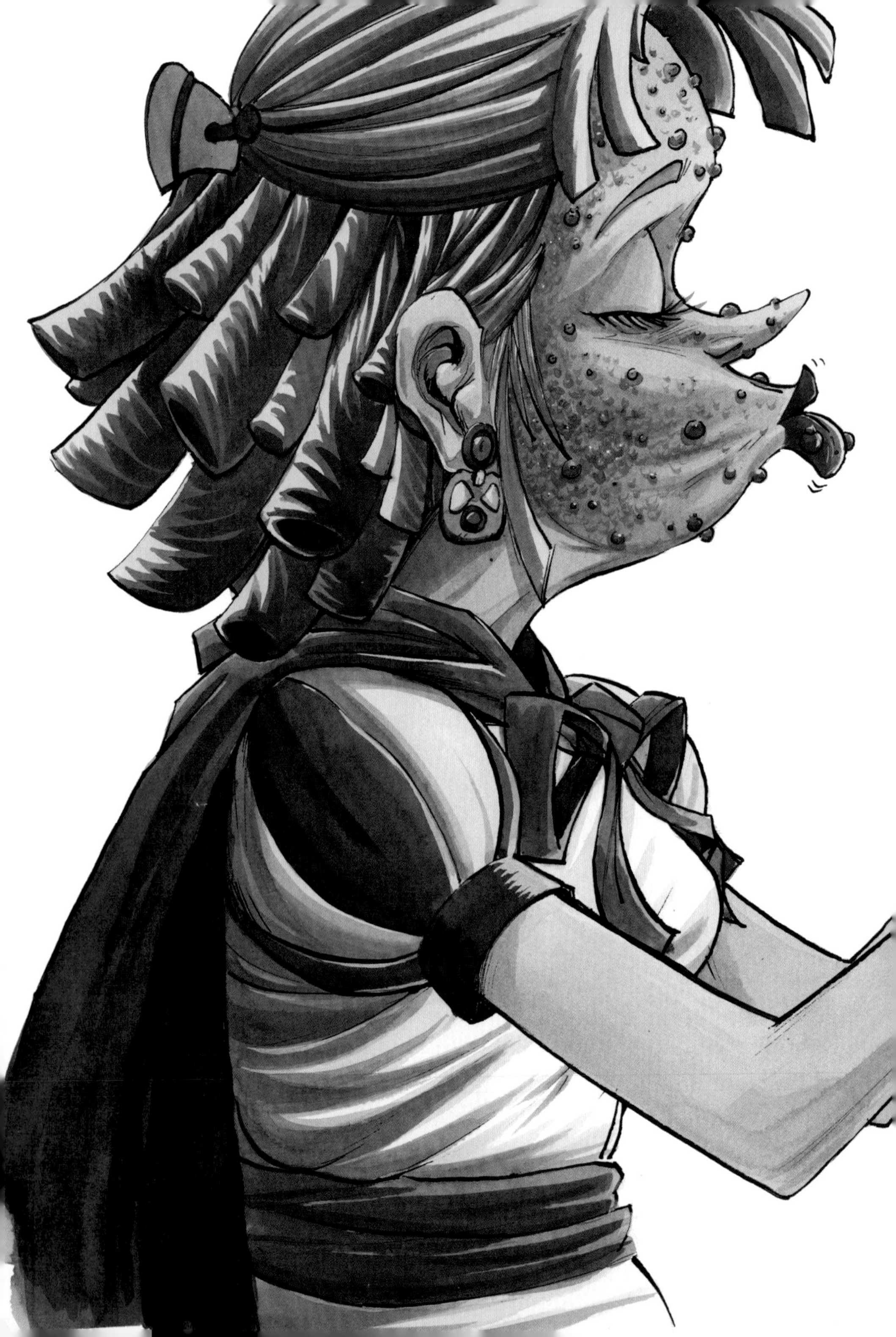

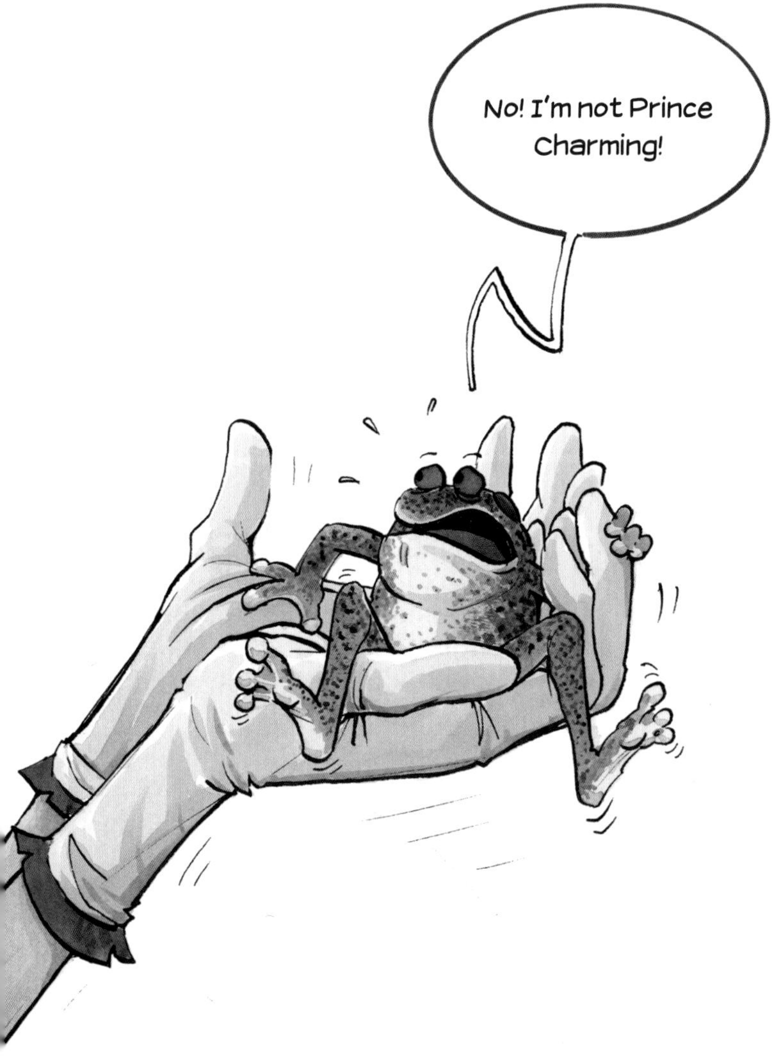
No! I'm not Prince Charming!

Toads can't actually spread warts to humans.

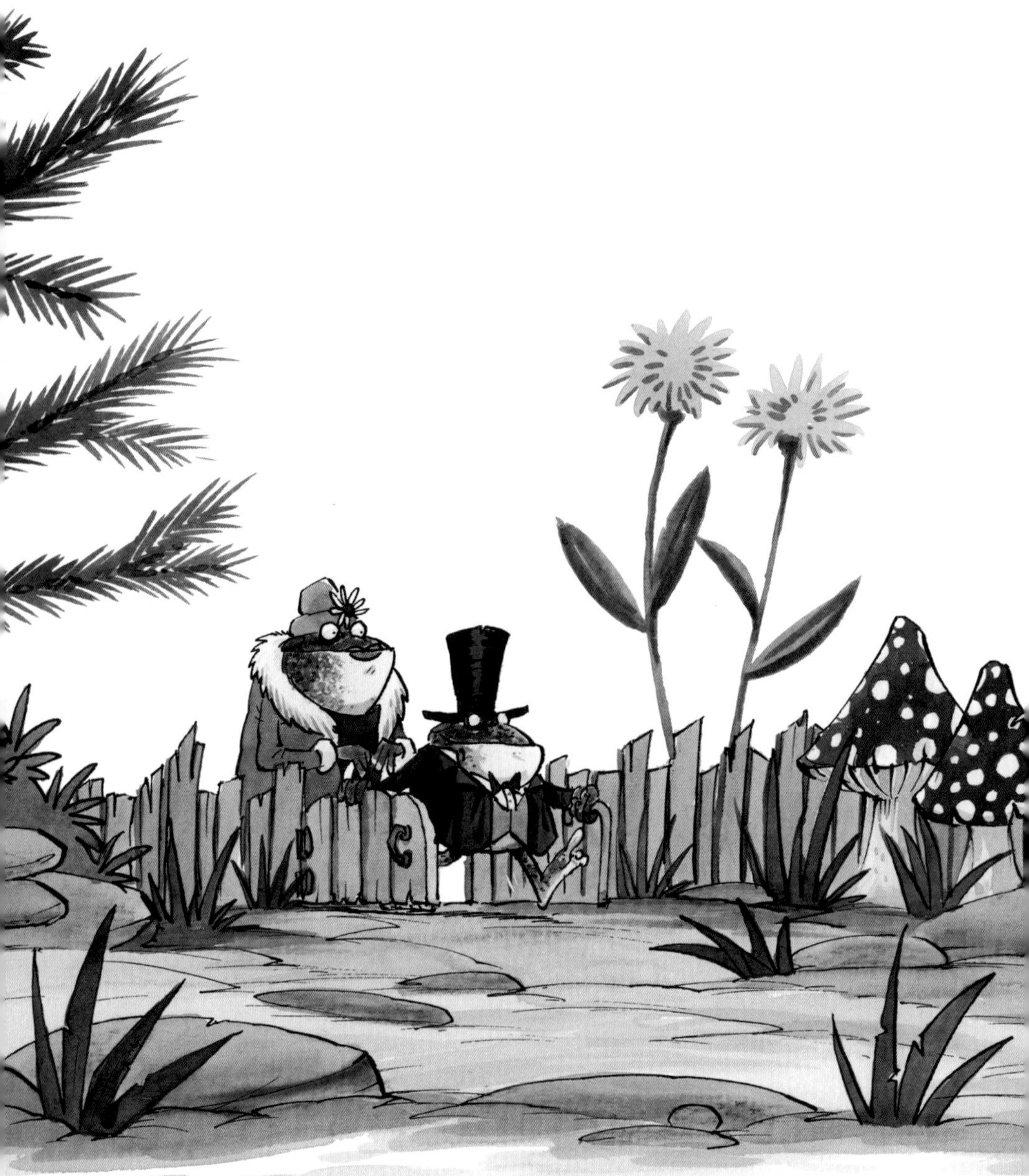

Toads are **nocturnal**. During the day, they hide out in sombre and humid spots to protect themselves from the sun and from **predators.**

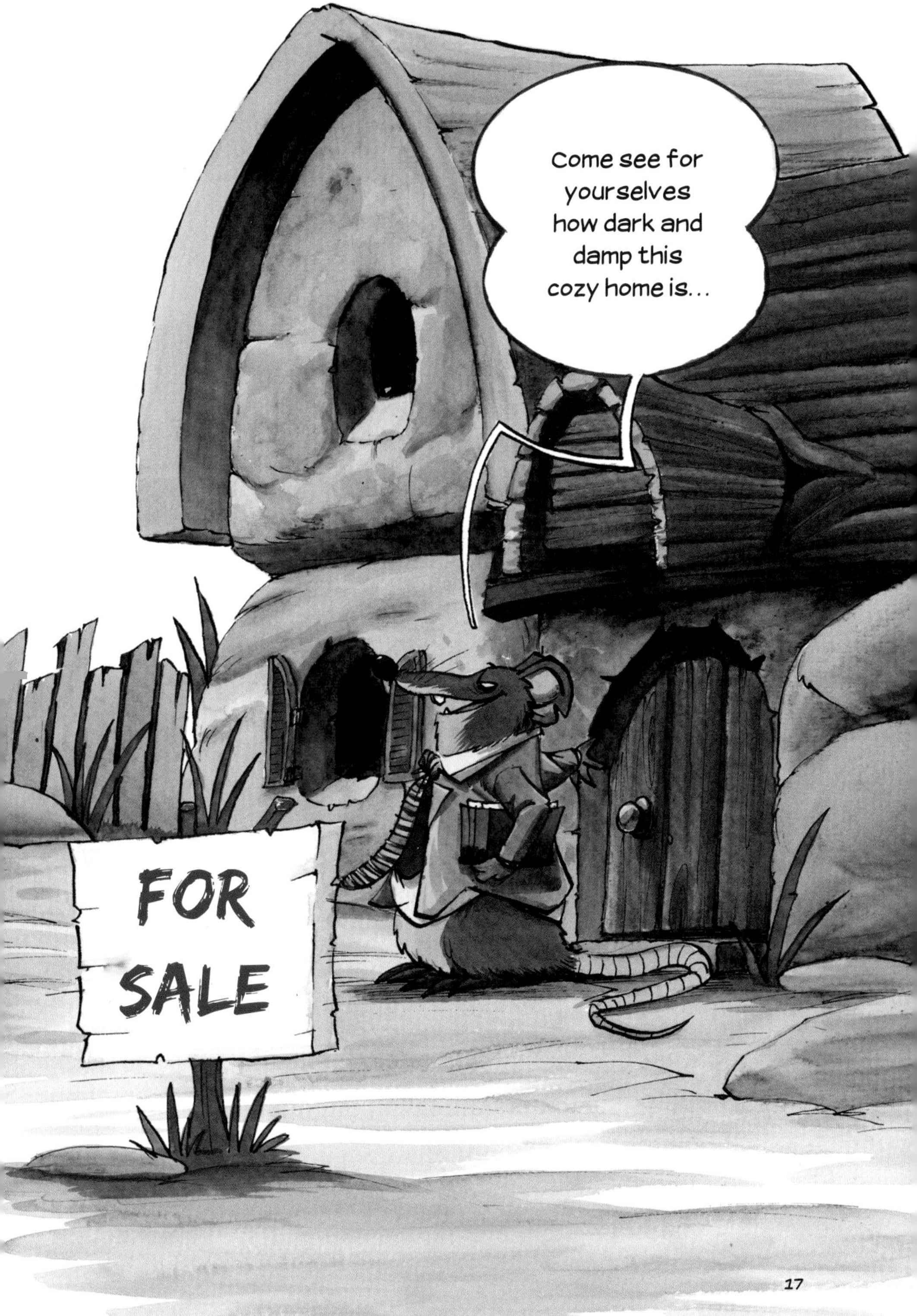
Come see for yourselves how dark and damp this cozy home is...
FOR SALE

Toads primarily eat insects, spiders, slugs and worms. They play an important role in the environment by eating so many pesky insects.

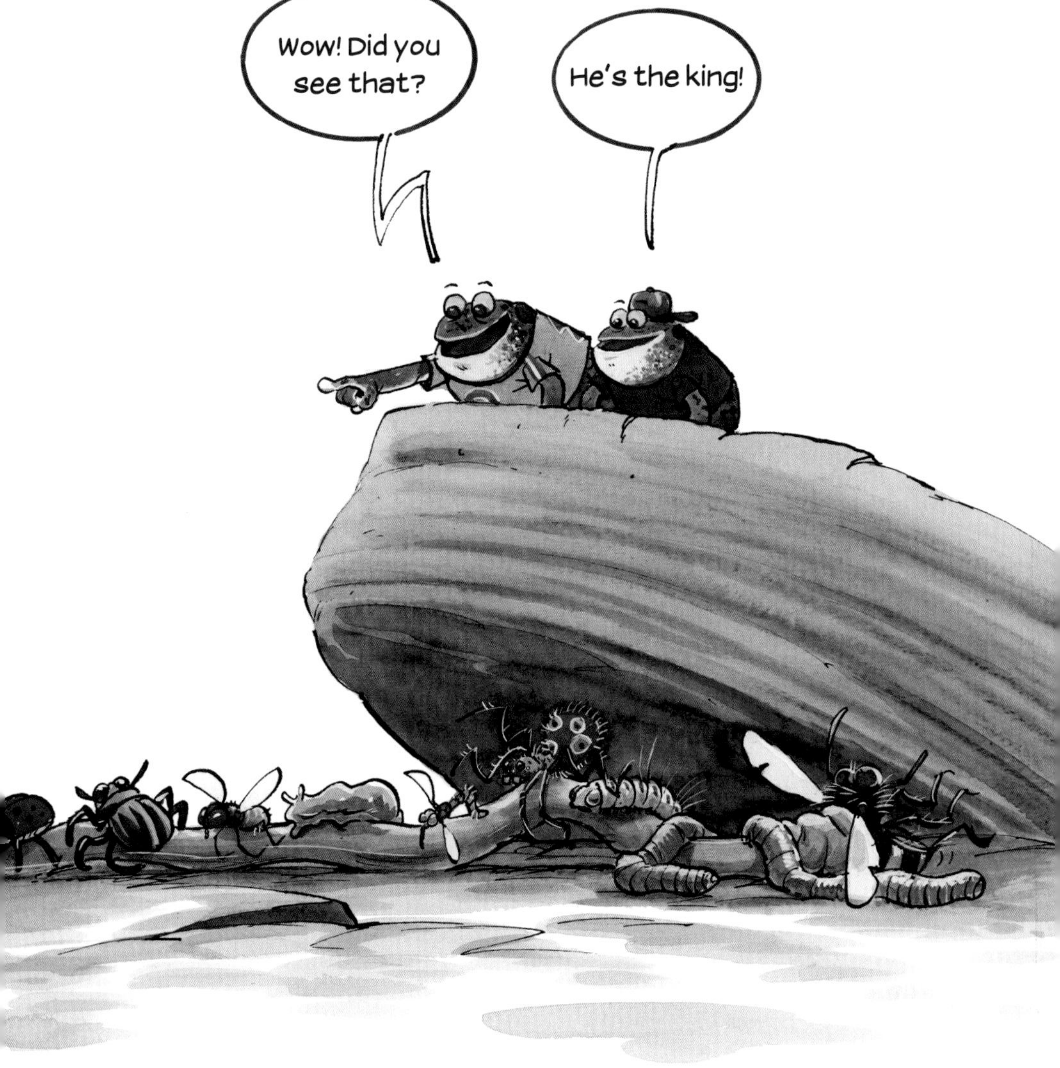
Wow! Did you see that?
He's the king!

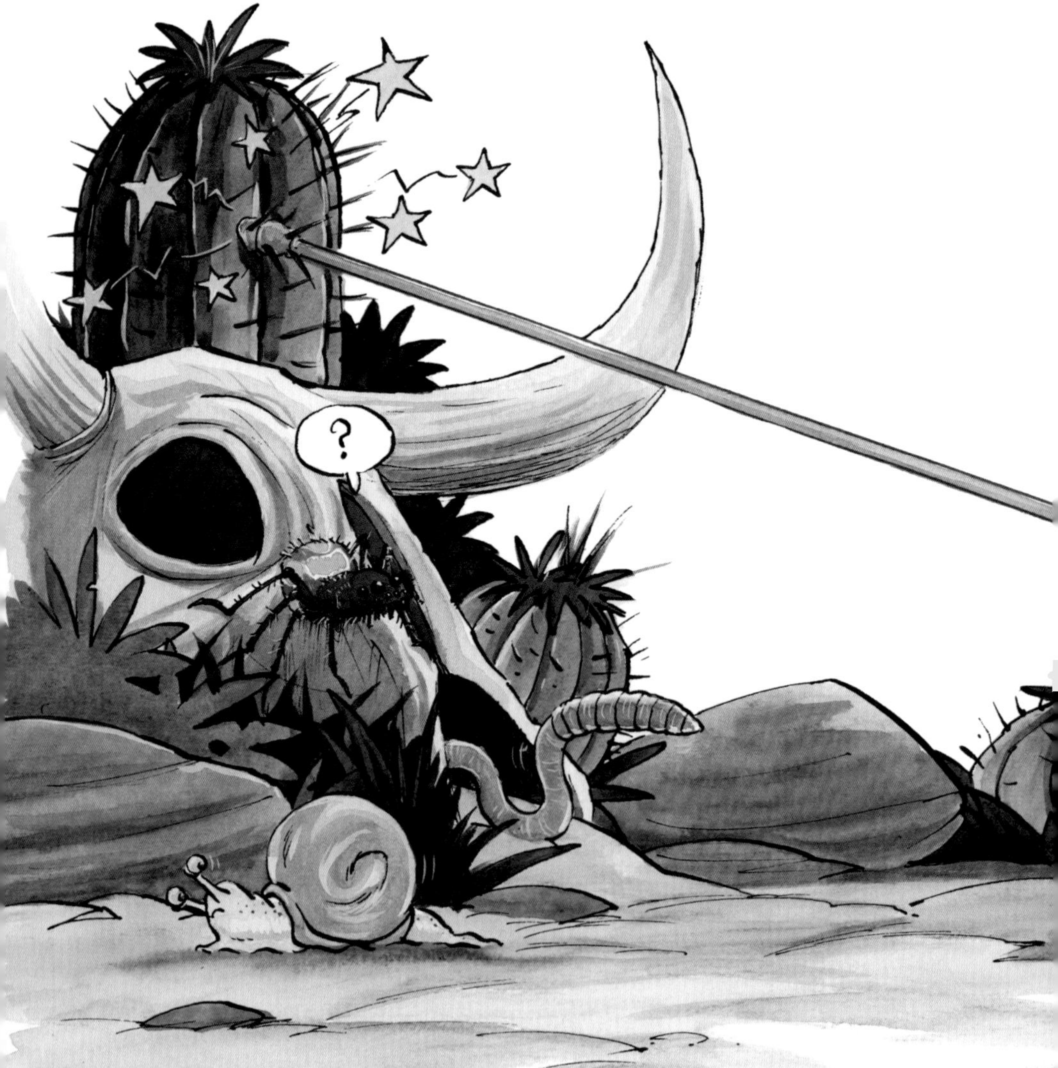
?

They catch their **prey** with their long, sticky tongues and swallow them whole. They whip out their tongues so fast that insects barely have any chance of escaping.

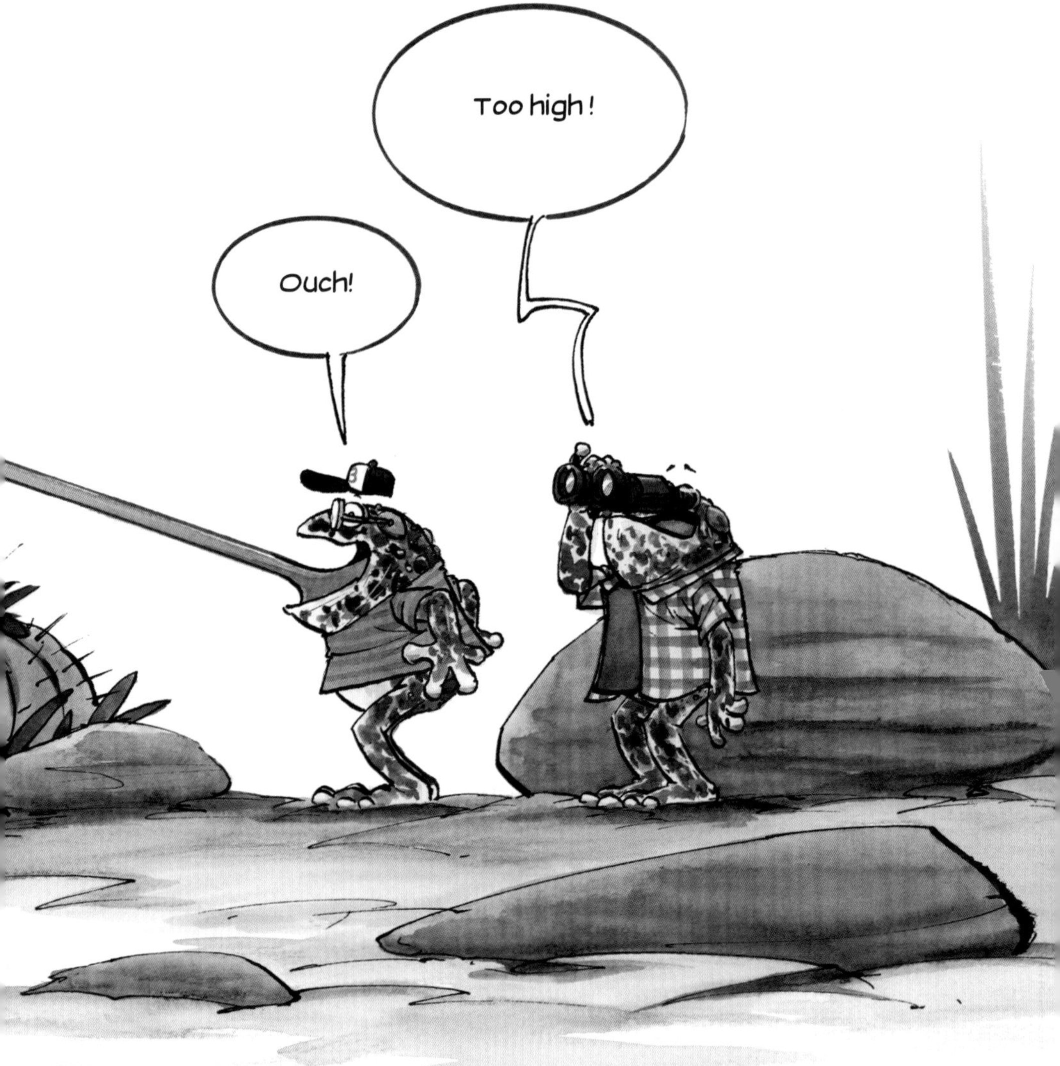
Ouch!
Too high!

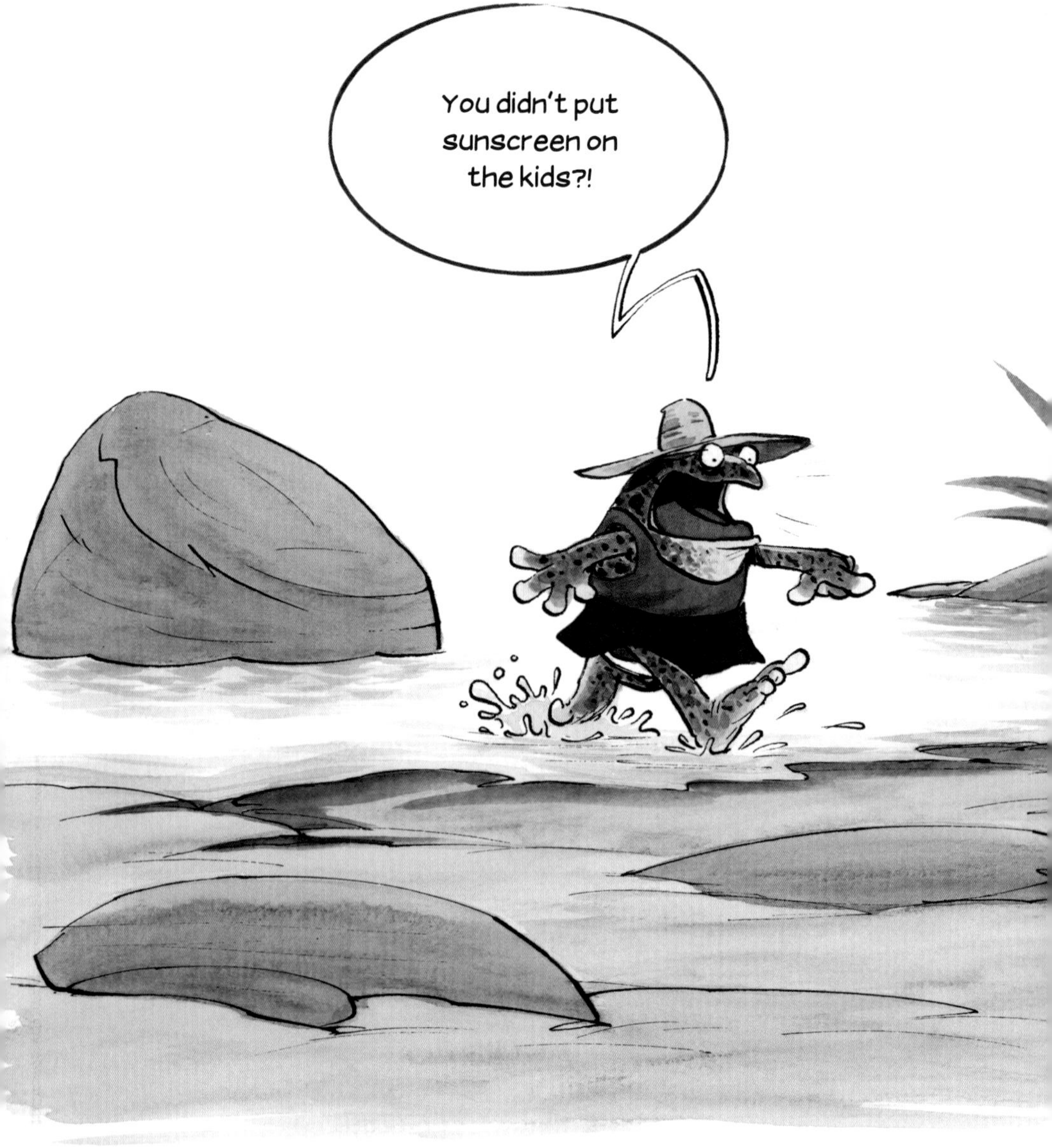
You didn't put sunscreen on the kids?!

The toad is a cold-blooded animal. Its body temperature varies according to its environment.

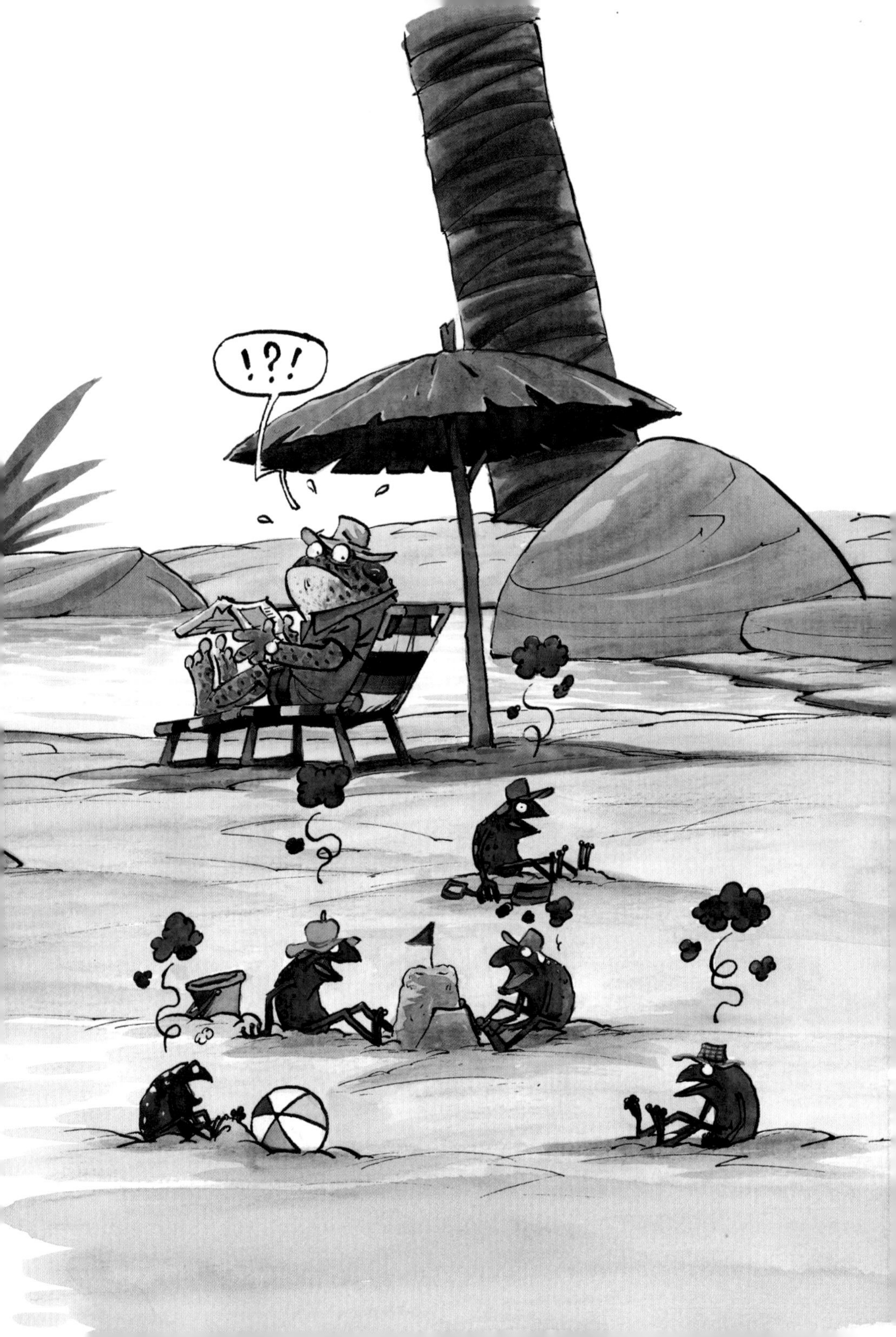
!?!

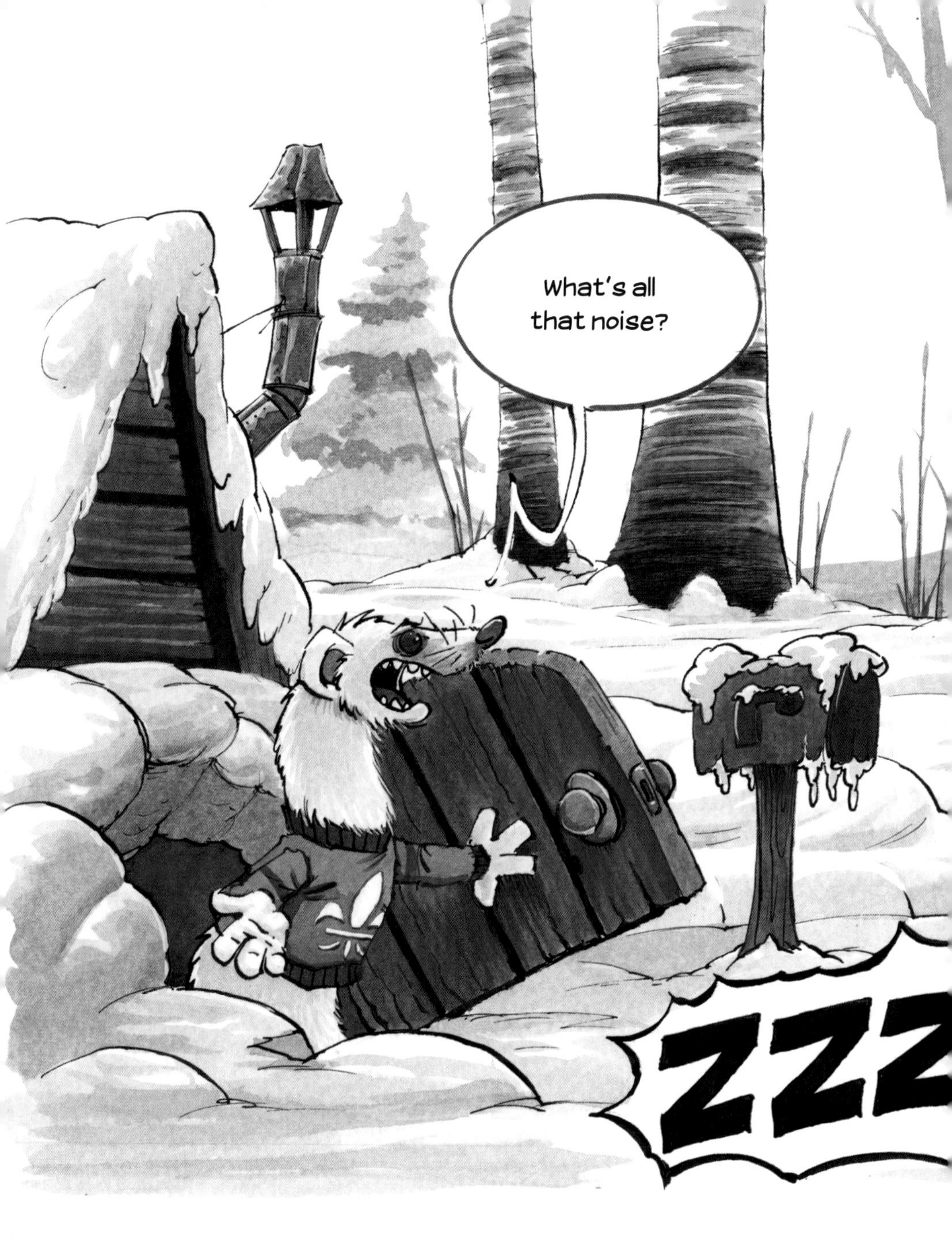
What's all that noise?
ZZZ

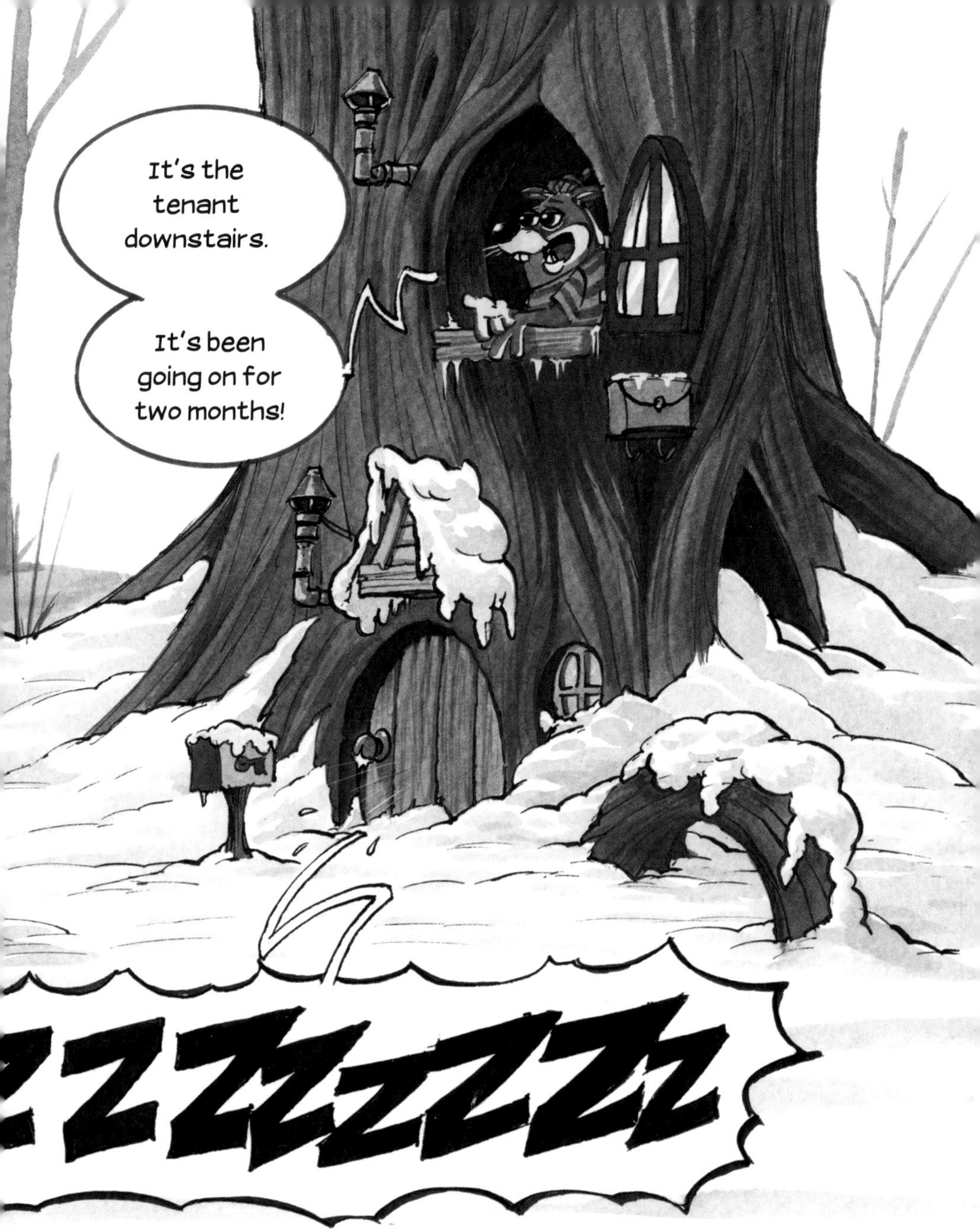
It's the tenant downstairs.
It's been going on for two months!
ZZZZZZZ

In temperate regions, toads hibernate. To ensure that they don't freeze, they burrow underground or under roots where the temperature is above freezing. Then, they fall into a state of **torpor**, or inactivity.

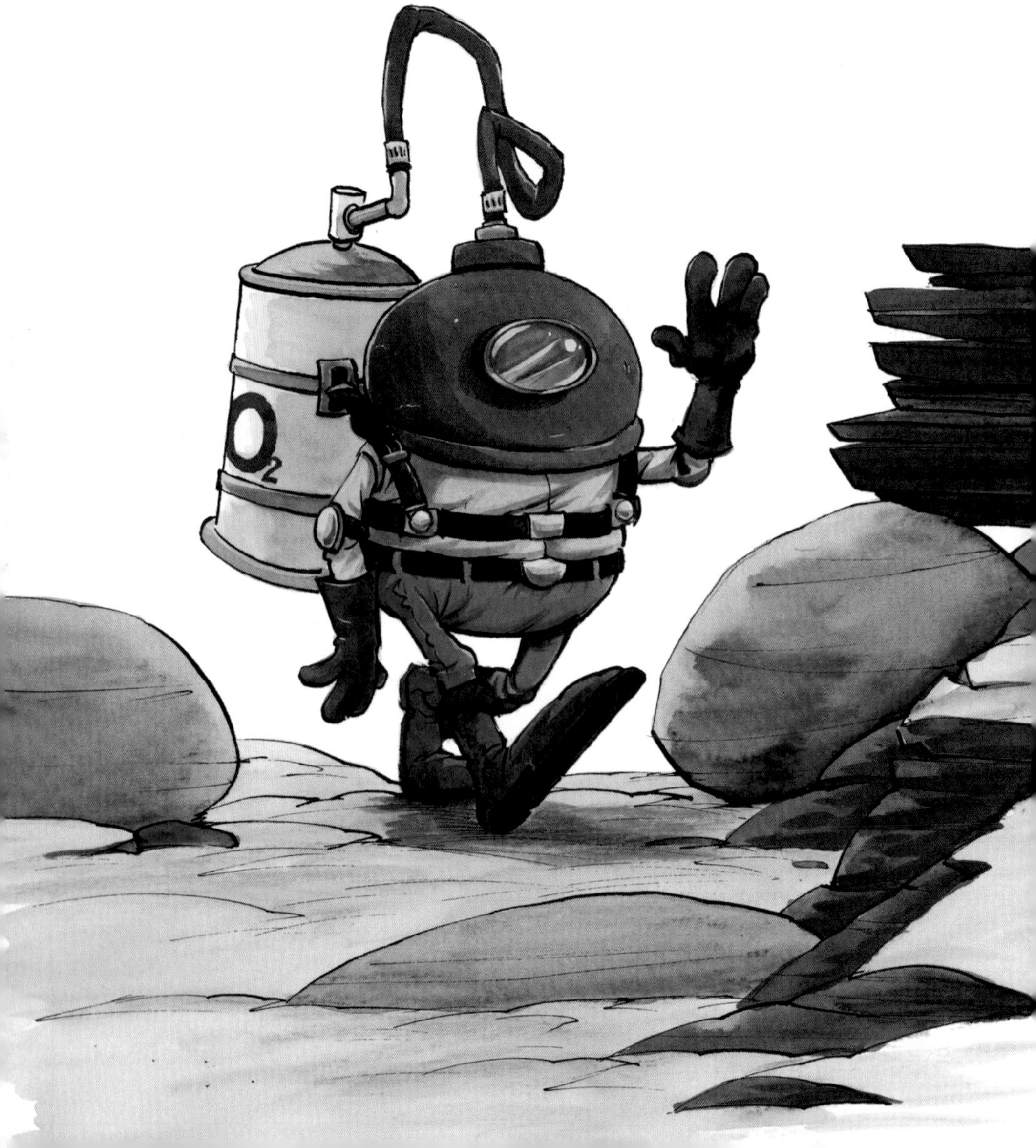
O_2

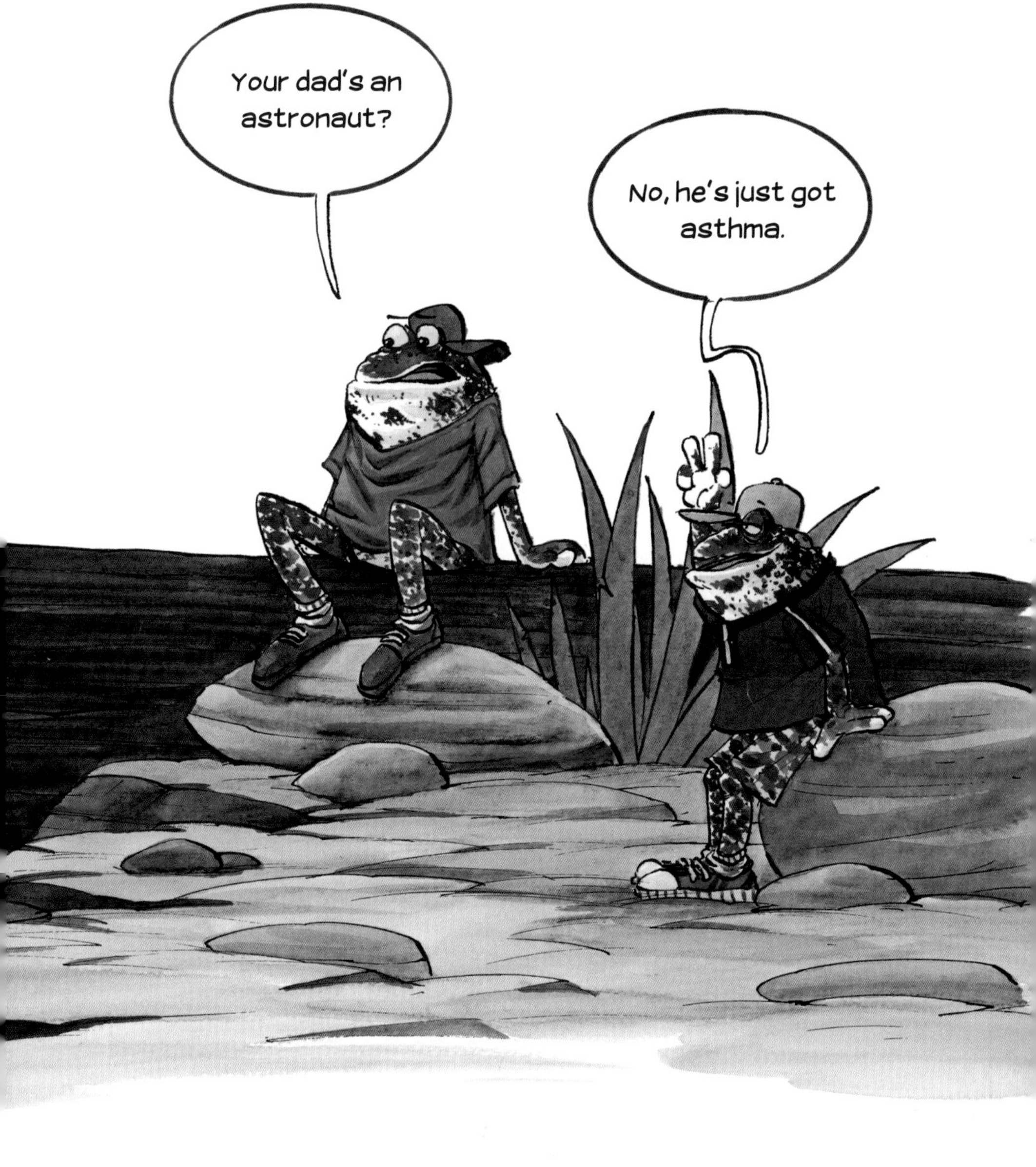
Your dad's an astronaut?
No, he's just got asthma.

Adult toads breathe through their lungs as well as their skin.

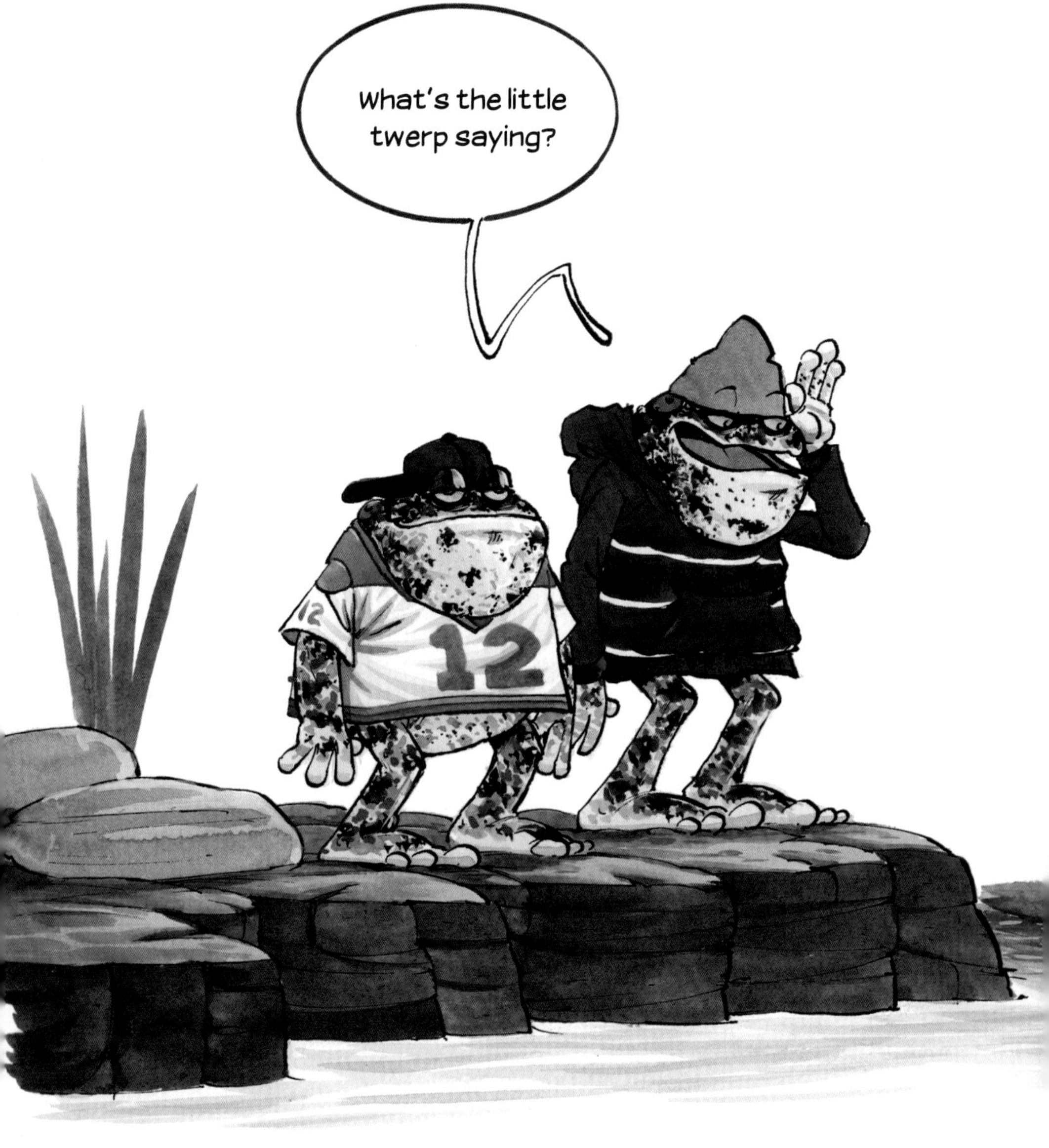
What's the little twerp saying?
12

Toads are **amphibians**. They live the first half of their lives in the water, and the other half on land.

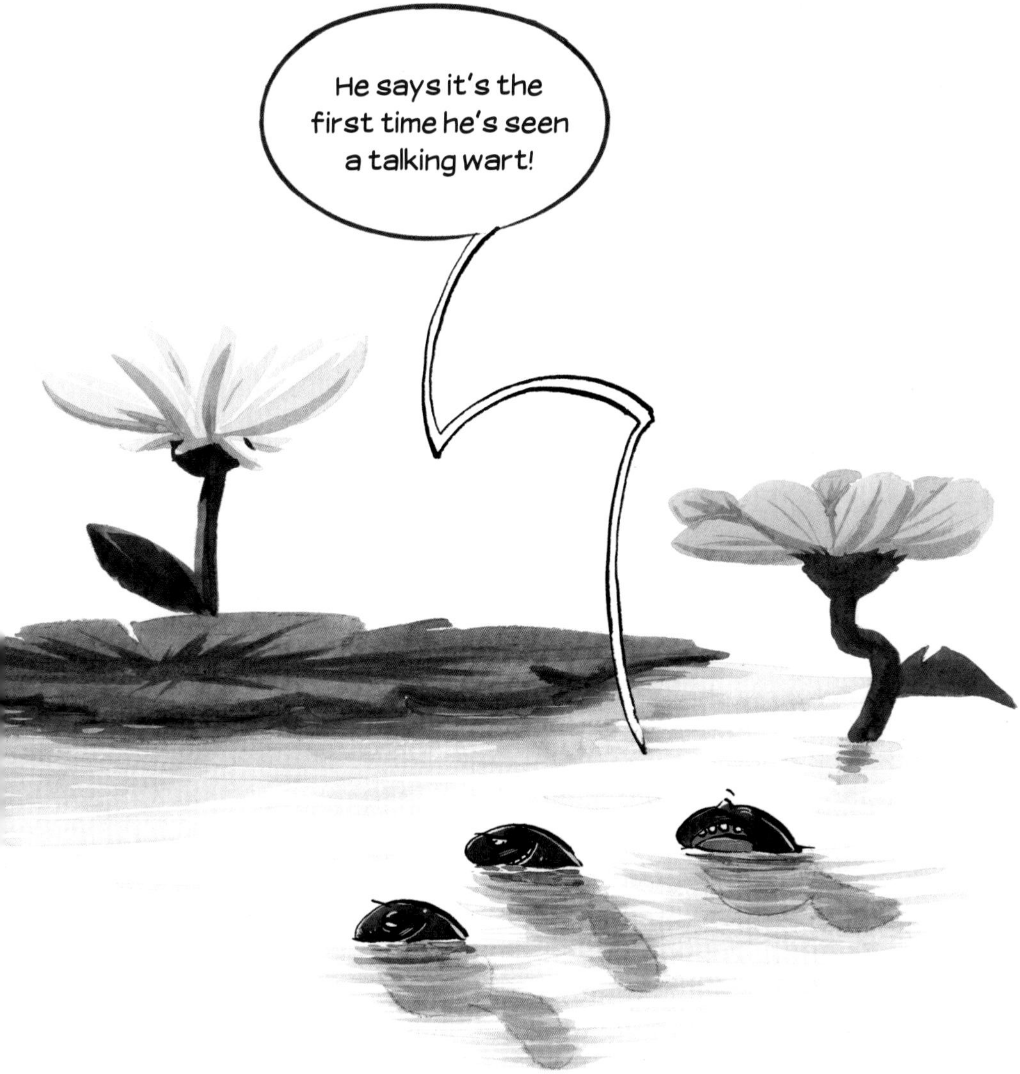
He says it's the first time he's seen a talking wart!

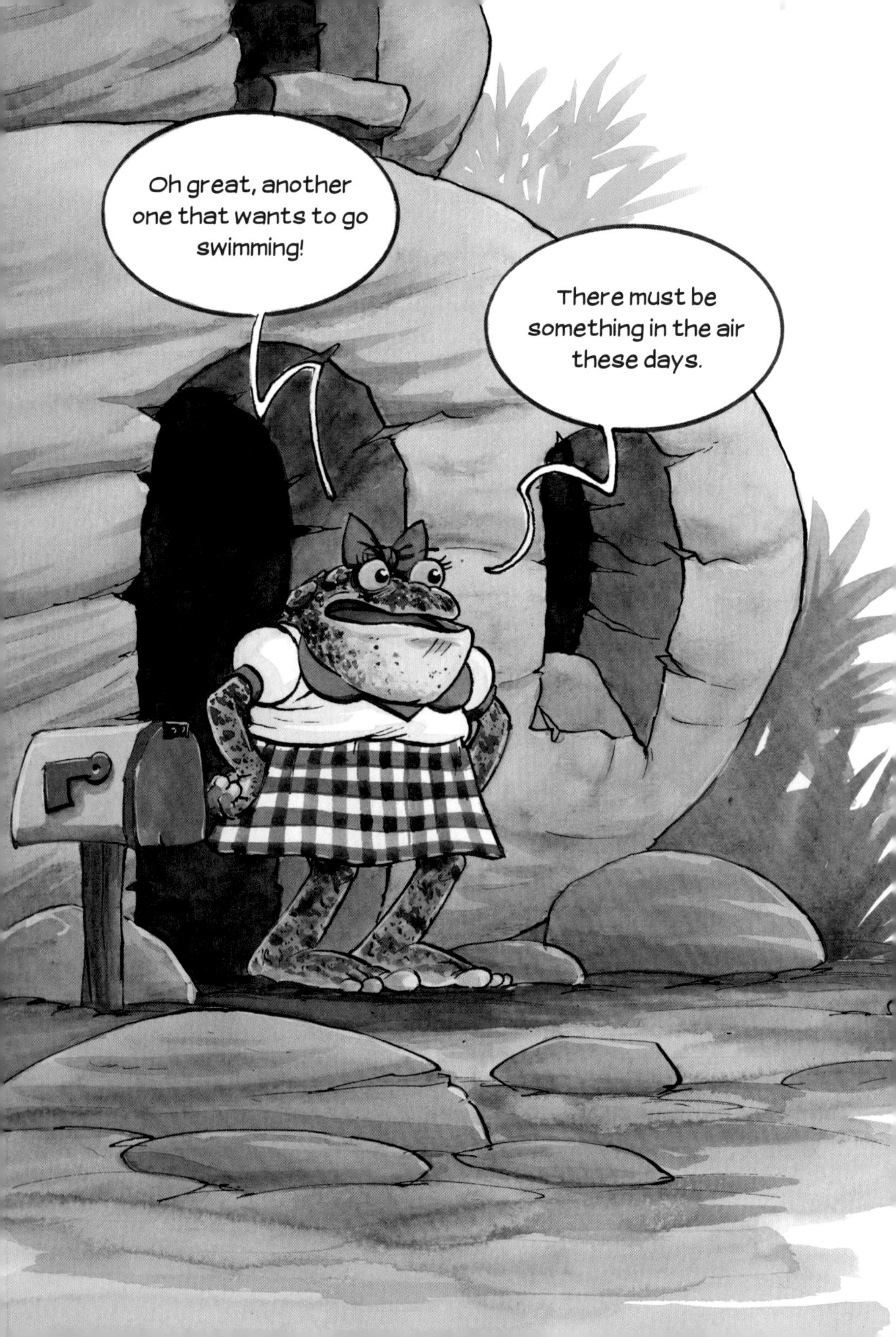
Oh great, another one that wants to go swimming!
There must be something in the air these days.

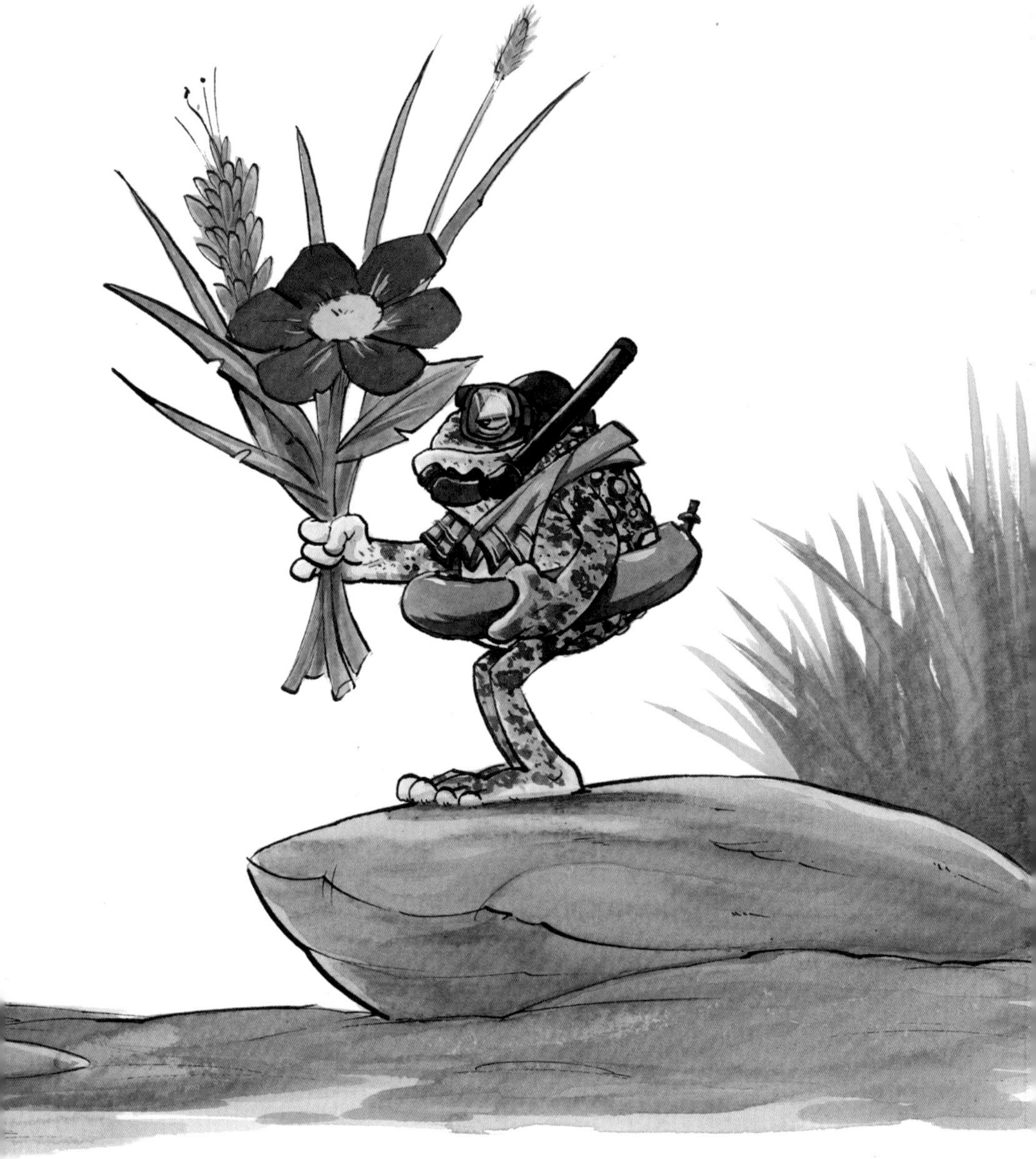

Adult toads are **terrestrial** animals. They only go in the water in the spring when it's time to mate. At this time of year, large numbers of toads can be found congregating in marshes and ponds.

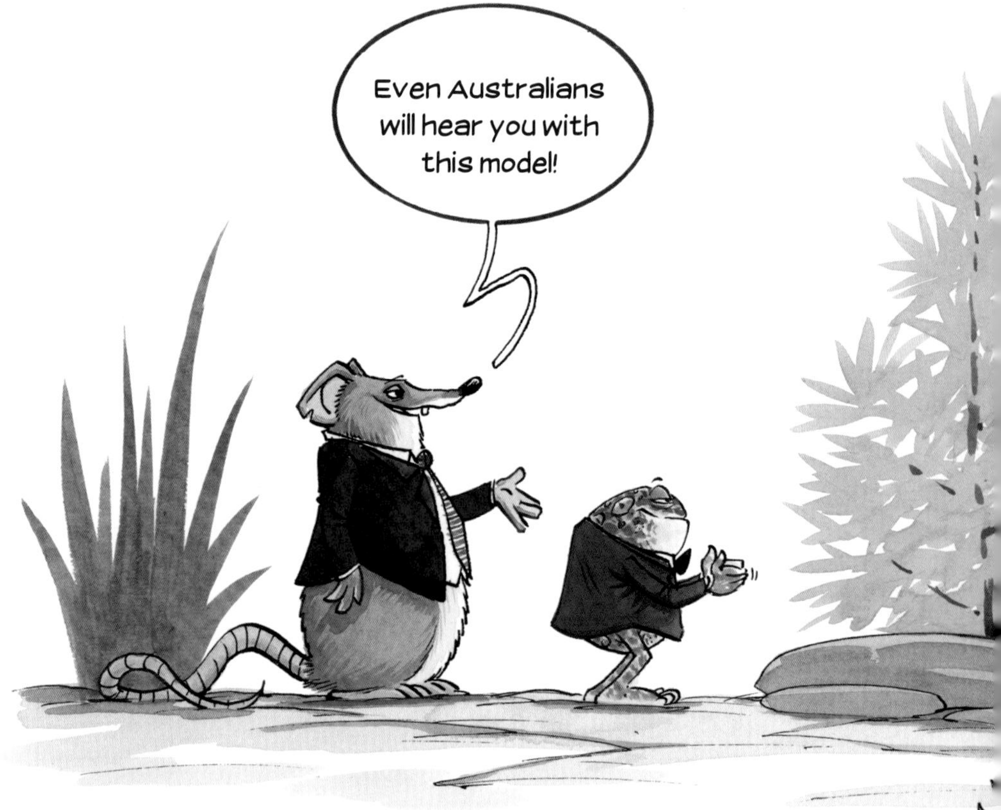
Even Australians
will hear you with
this model!

During this mating period, males call females by singing to them. The song of the male toad can be heard for kilometres around.

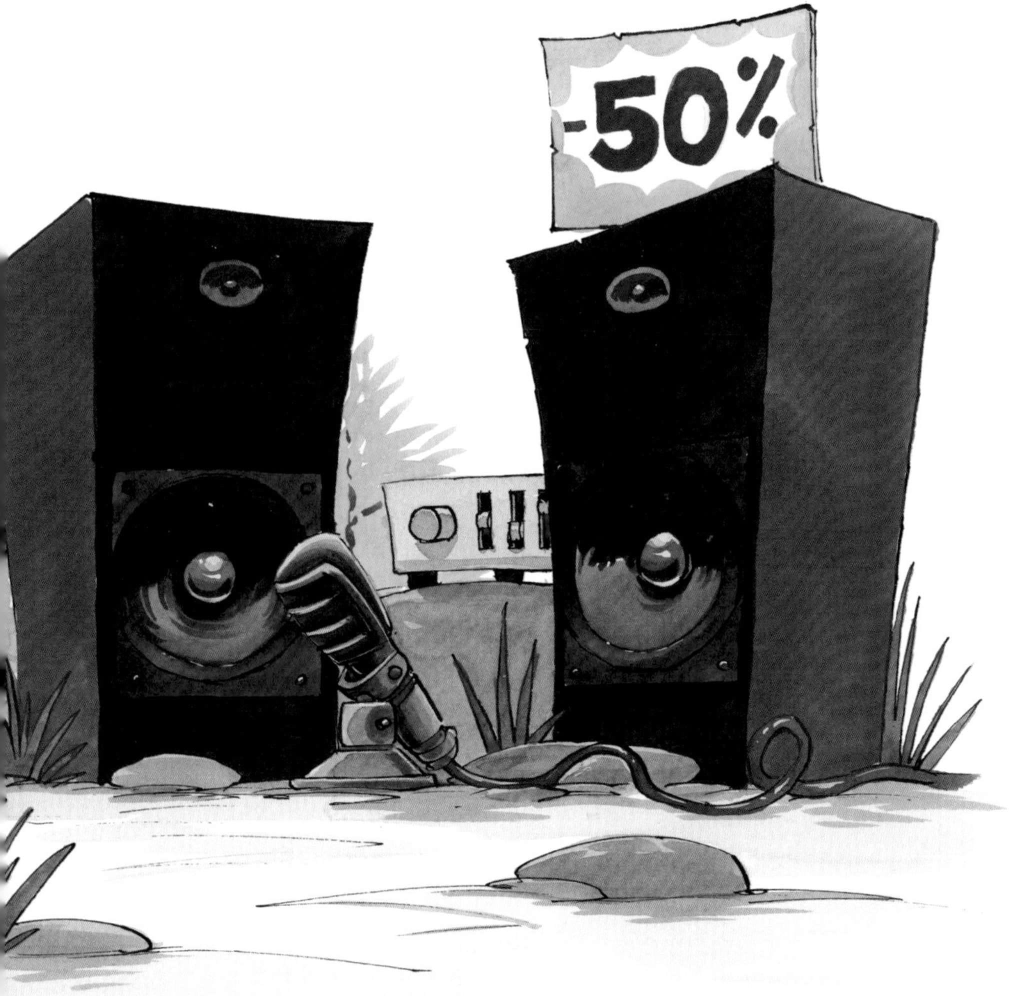
-50%

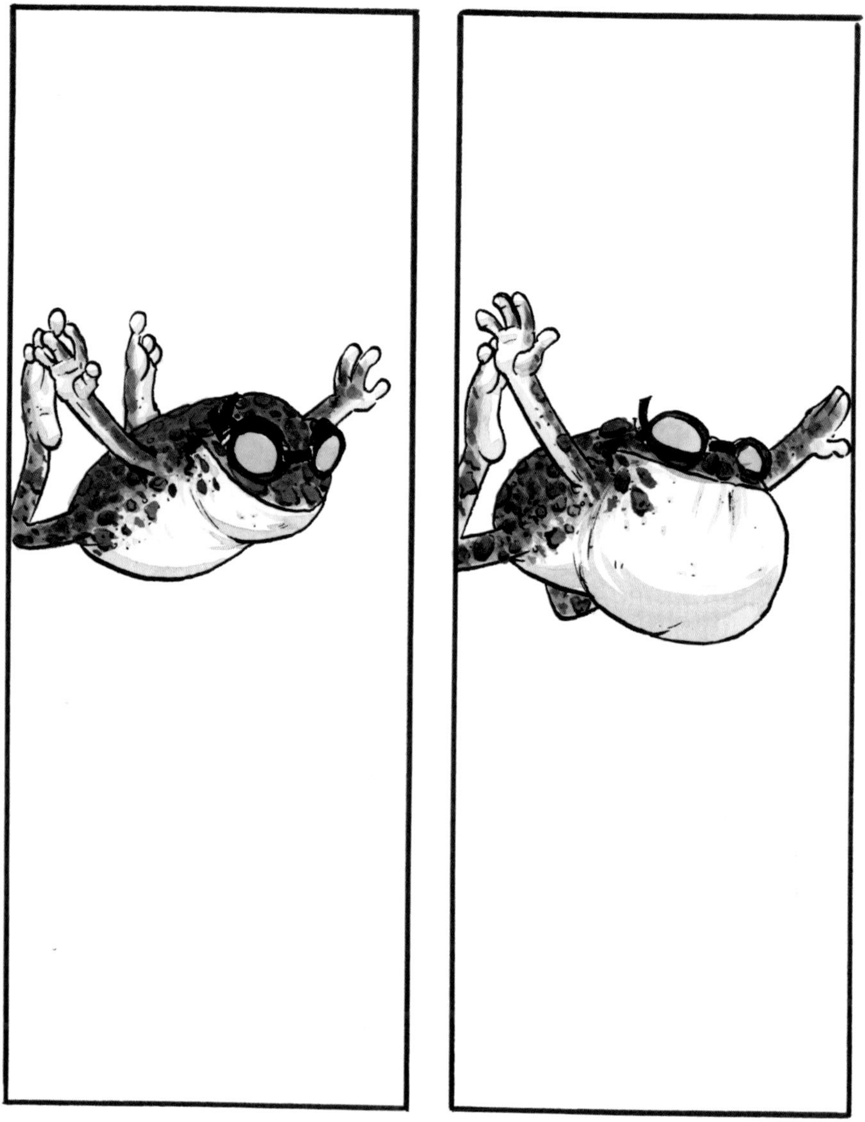

Only males have pouches under their throats. To produce its calls, the toad swells the vocal sac, which acts as a resonance box.

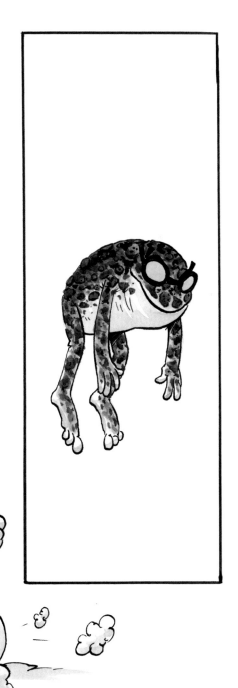

Boing!

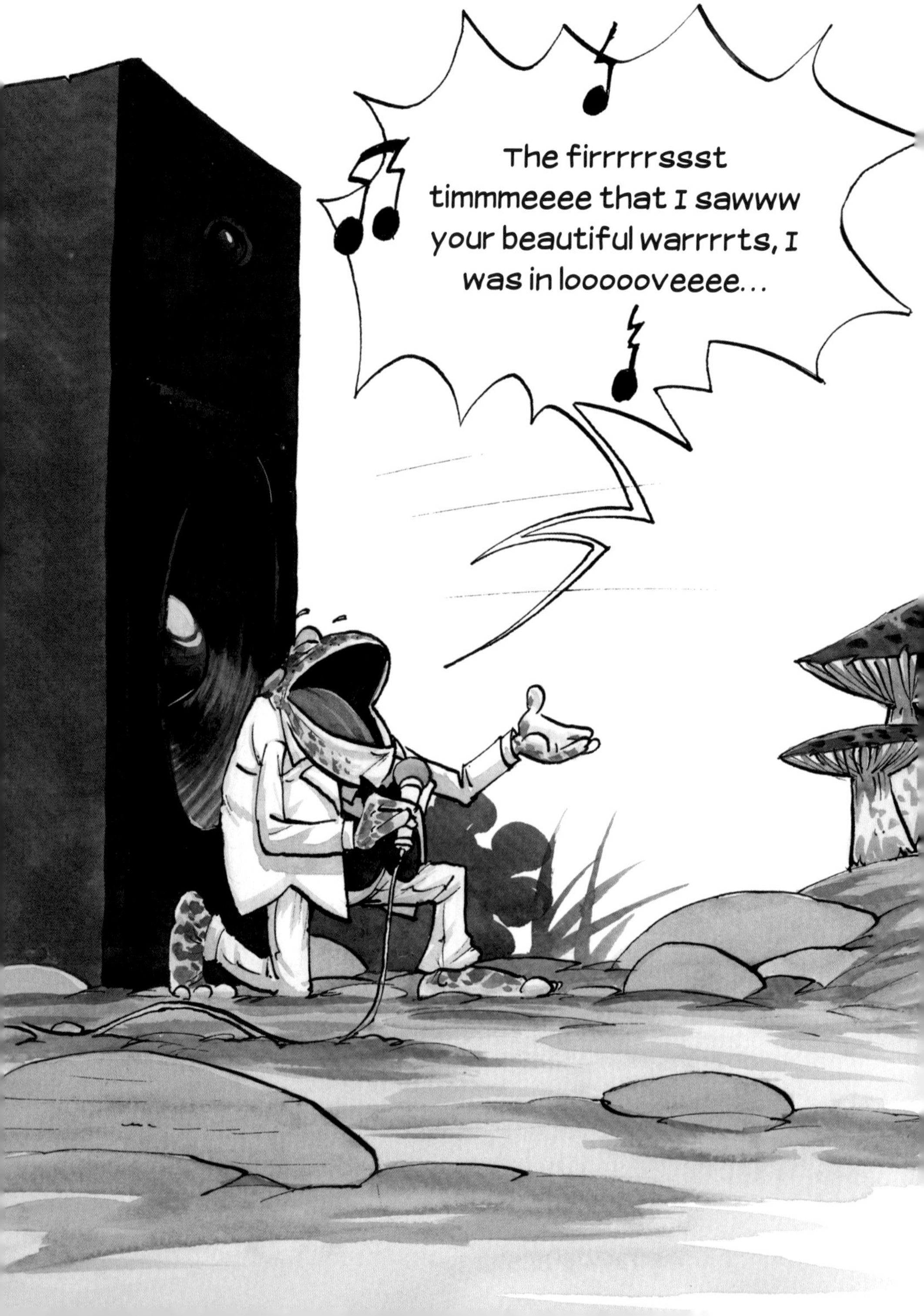
The firrrrrssst timmmeeee that I sawww your beautiful warrrrts, I was in loooooveeee...

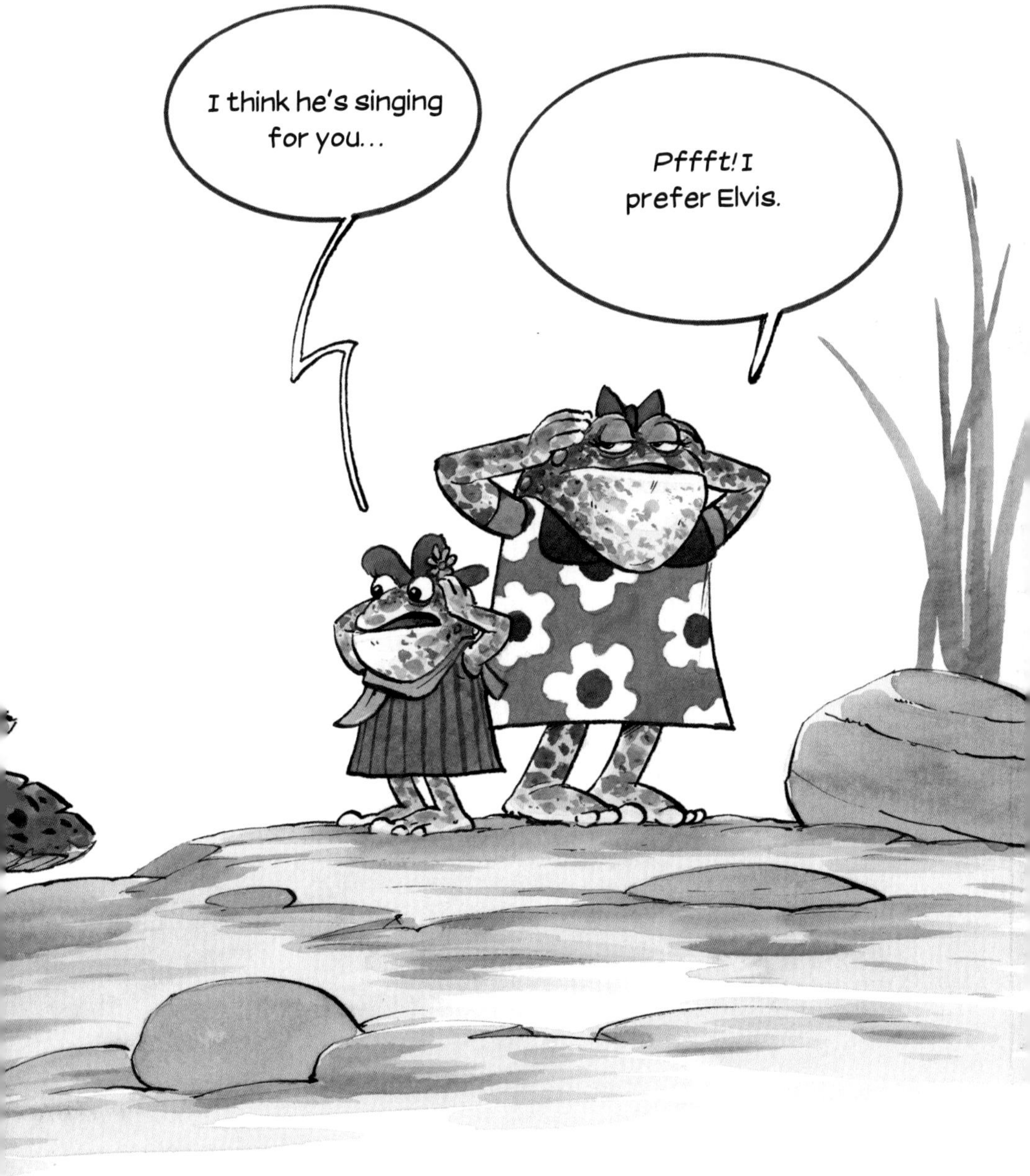
I think he's singing for you...
Pffft! I prefer Elvis.

Each species possesses a particular type of call. It is by this unique chorus that a female will recognize a toad of her own species.

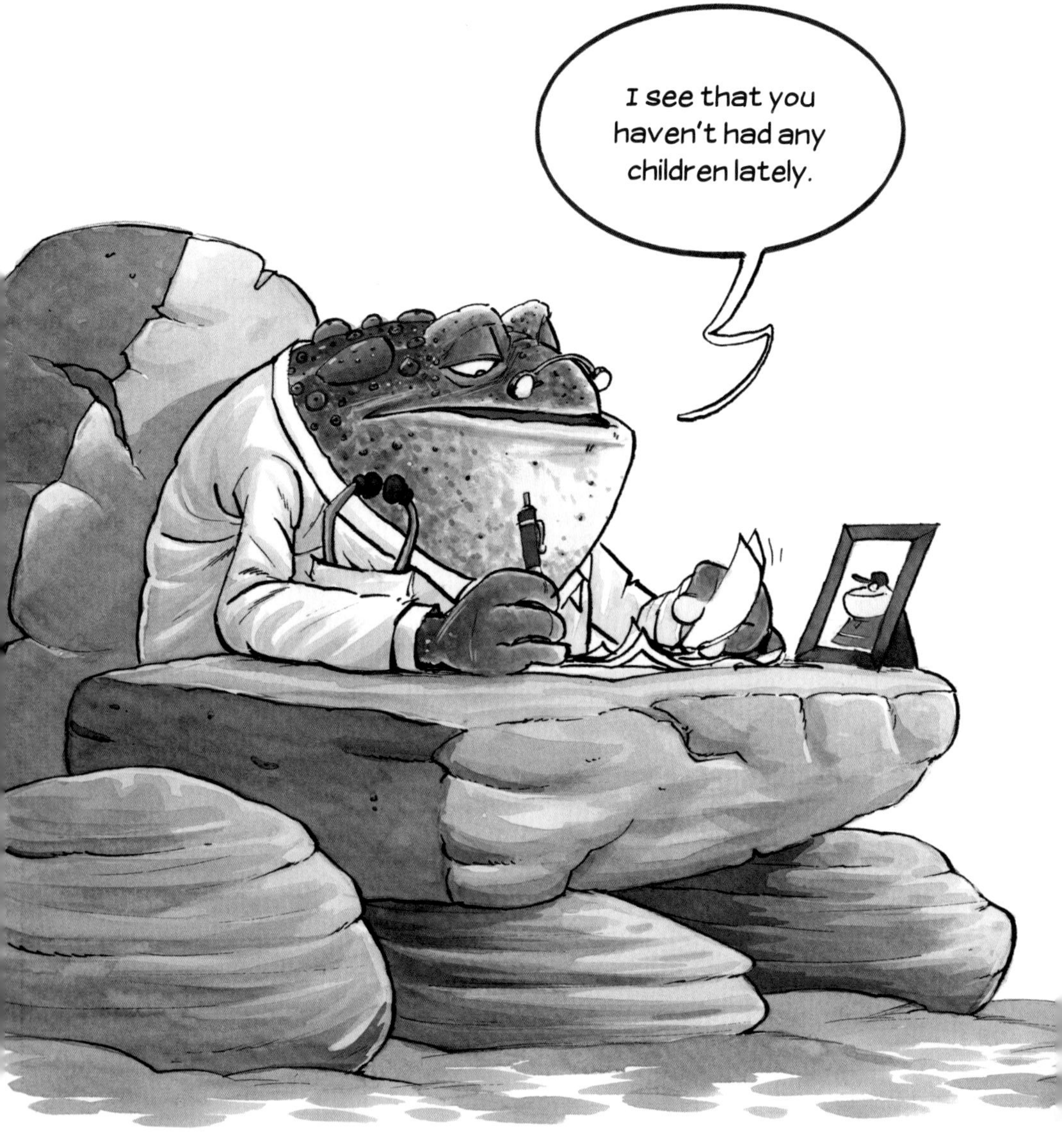
I see that you haven't had any children lately.

To mate, the male positions himself on the back of the female and grasps her tightly under the armpits. He can stay in this position for several days in a row until the female lays her eggs.

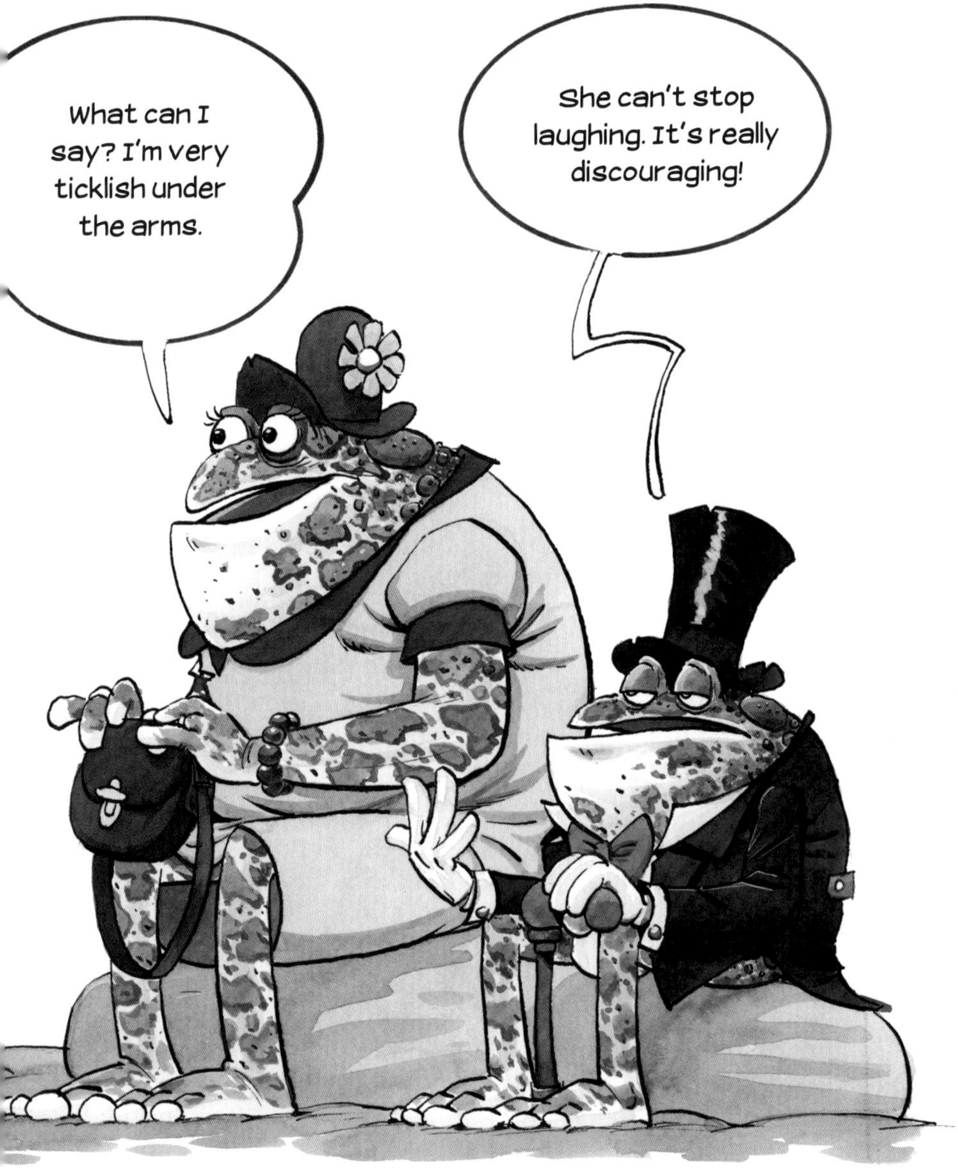
What can I say? I'm very ticklish under the arms.
She can't stop laughing. It's really discouraging!

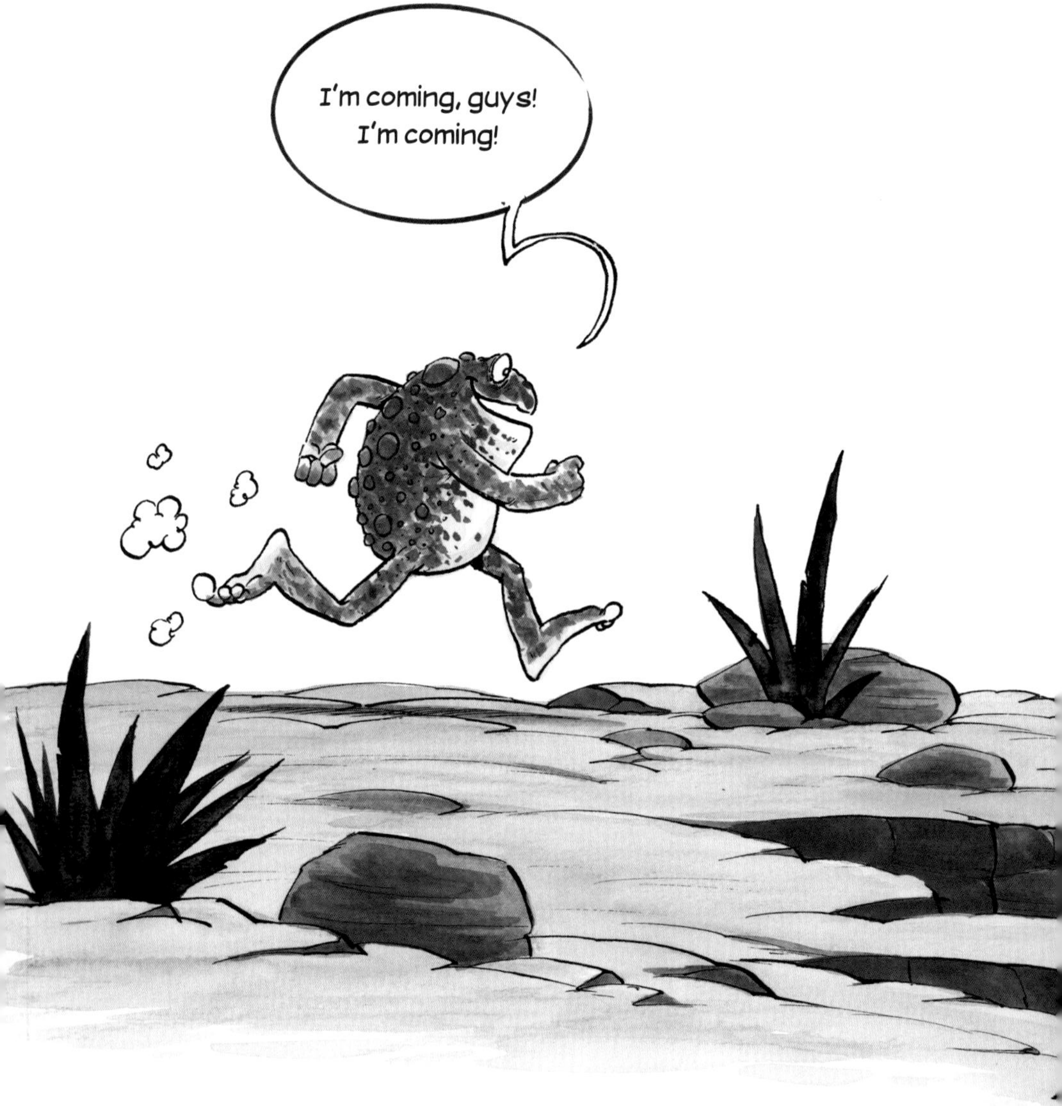
I'm coming, guys!
I'm coming!

Sometimes, several males will try to mate with the same female simultaneously. The enormous weight on her back can suffocate or drown her.

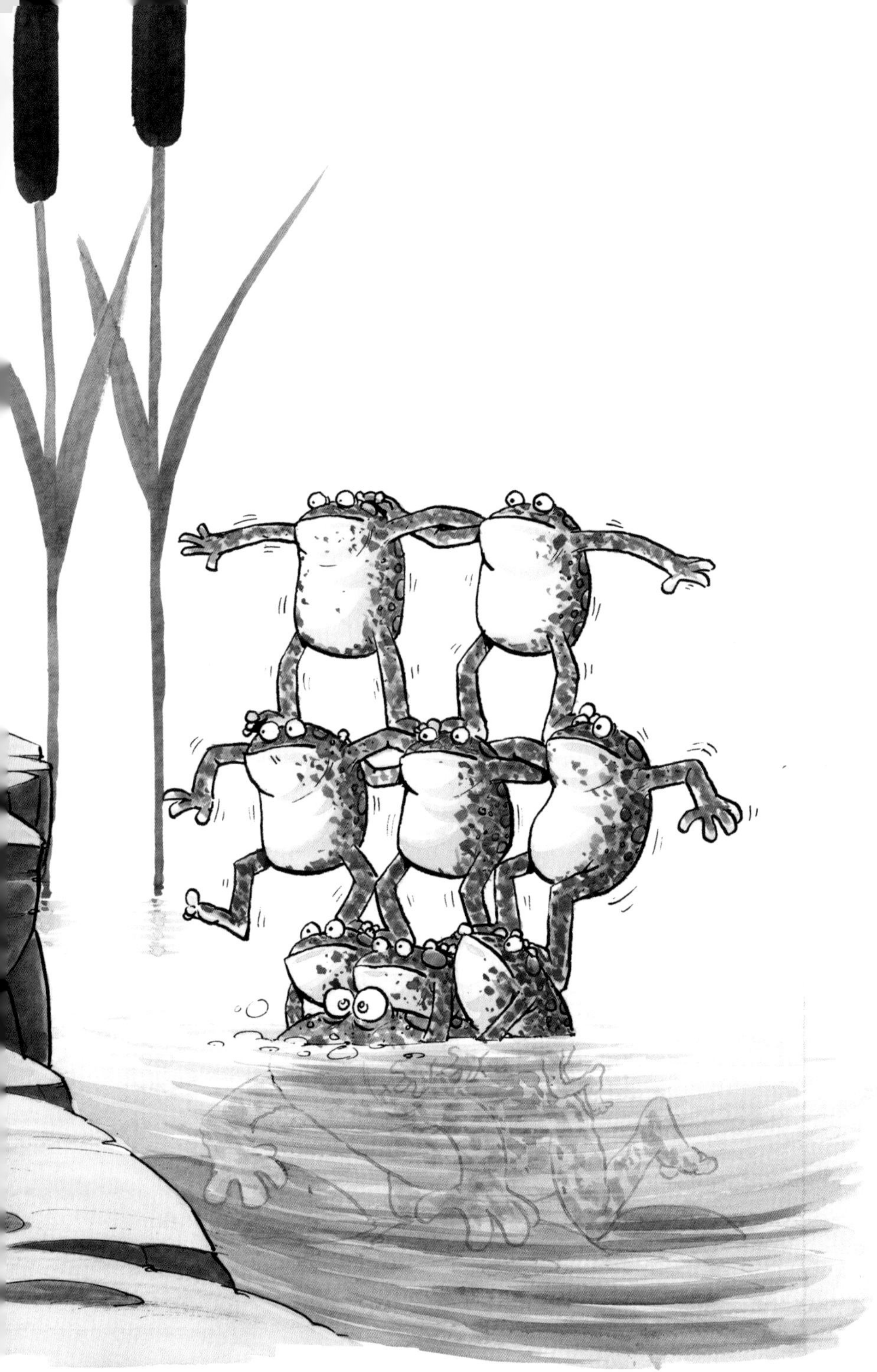

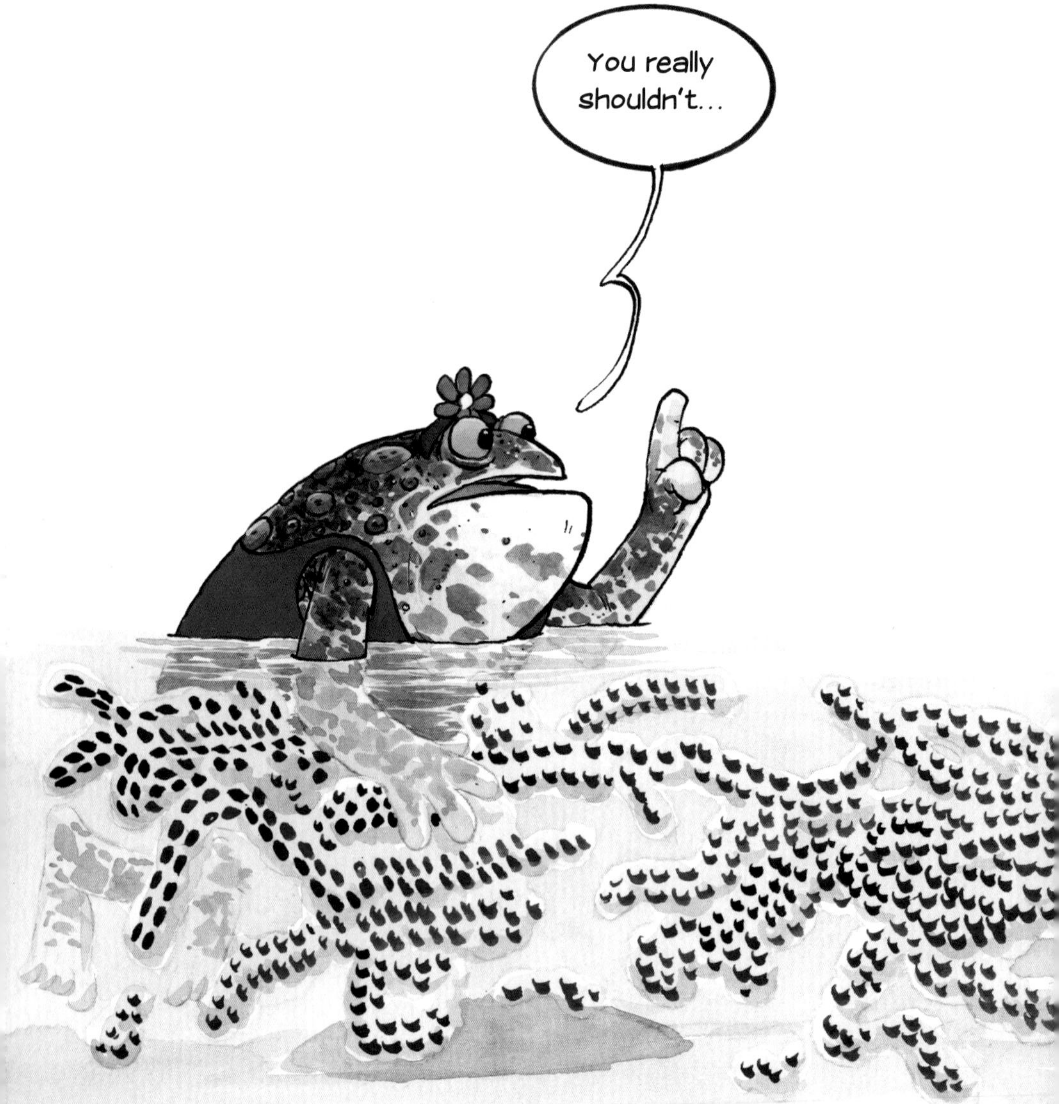
You really shouldn't...

At the exact same time as the female lays her eggs, the male liberates the semen that fertilizes them. Just like fish eggs, toad eggs don't have hard shells; they're protected by a gelatinous covering.

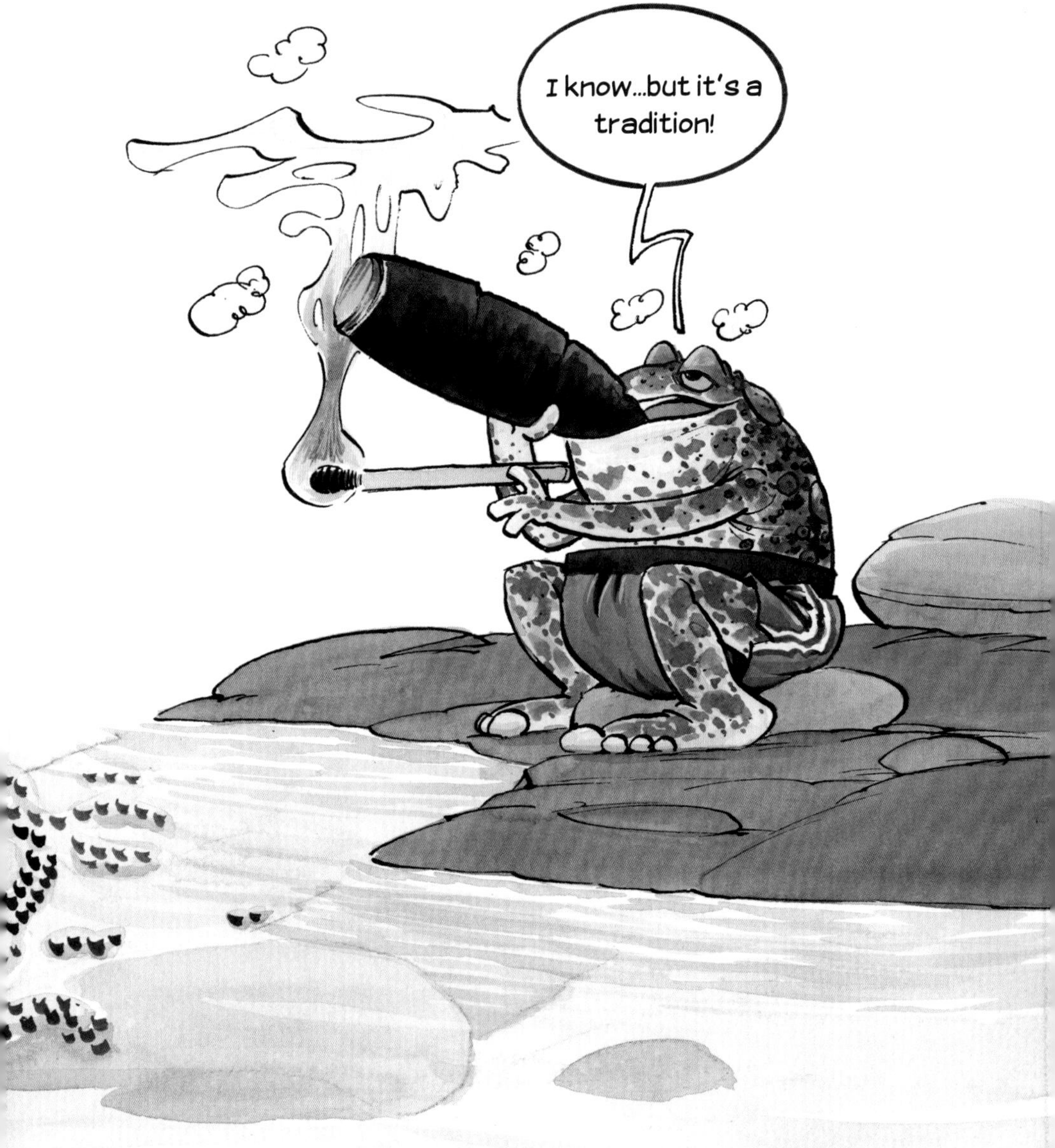
I know...but it's a tradition!

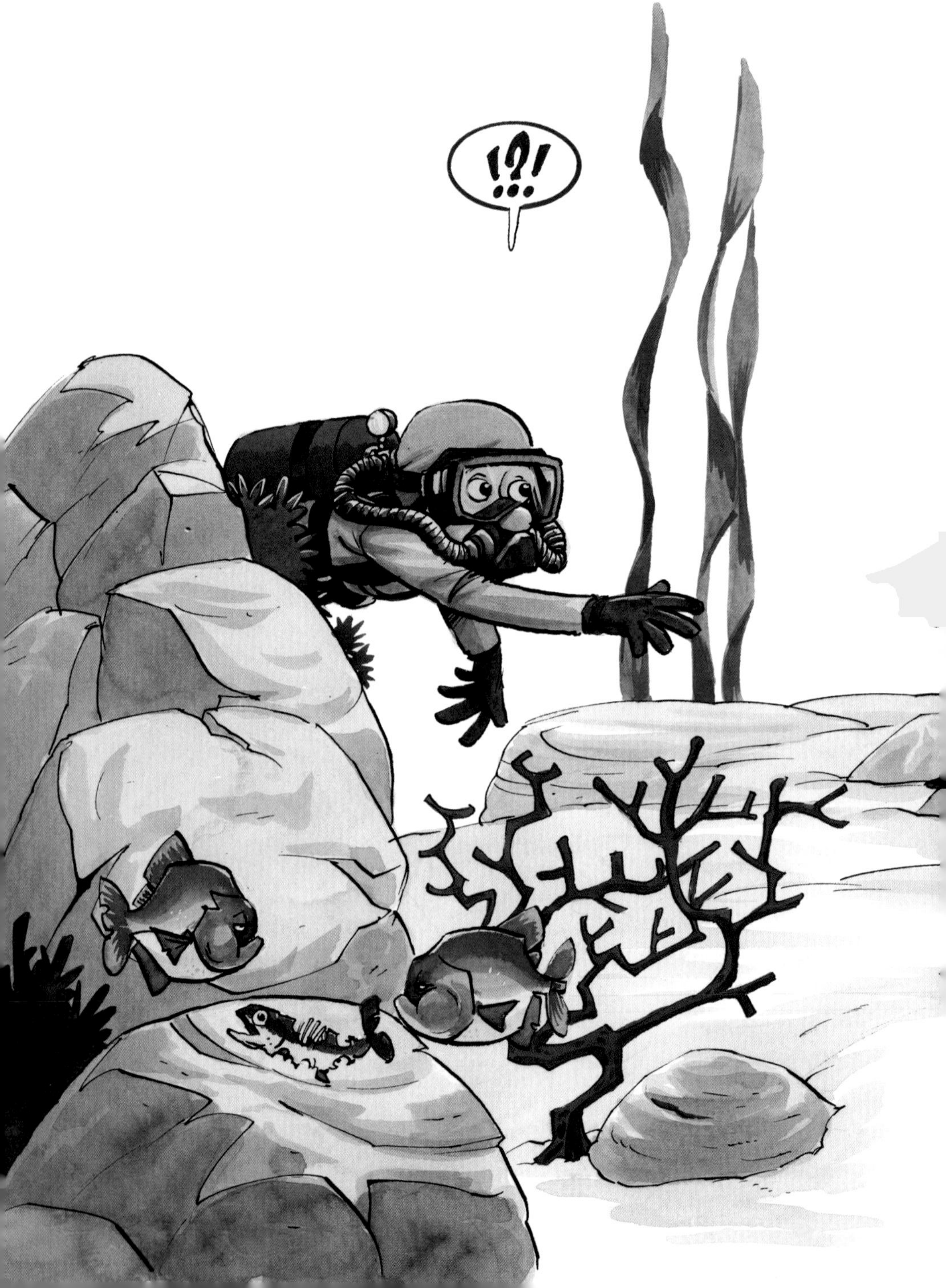
!?!

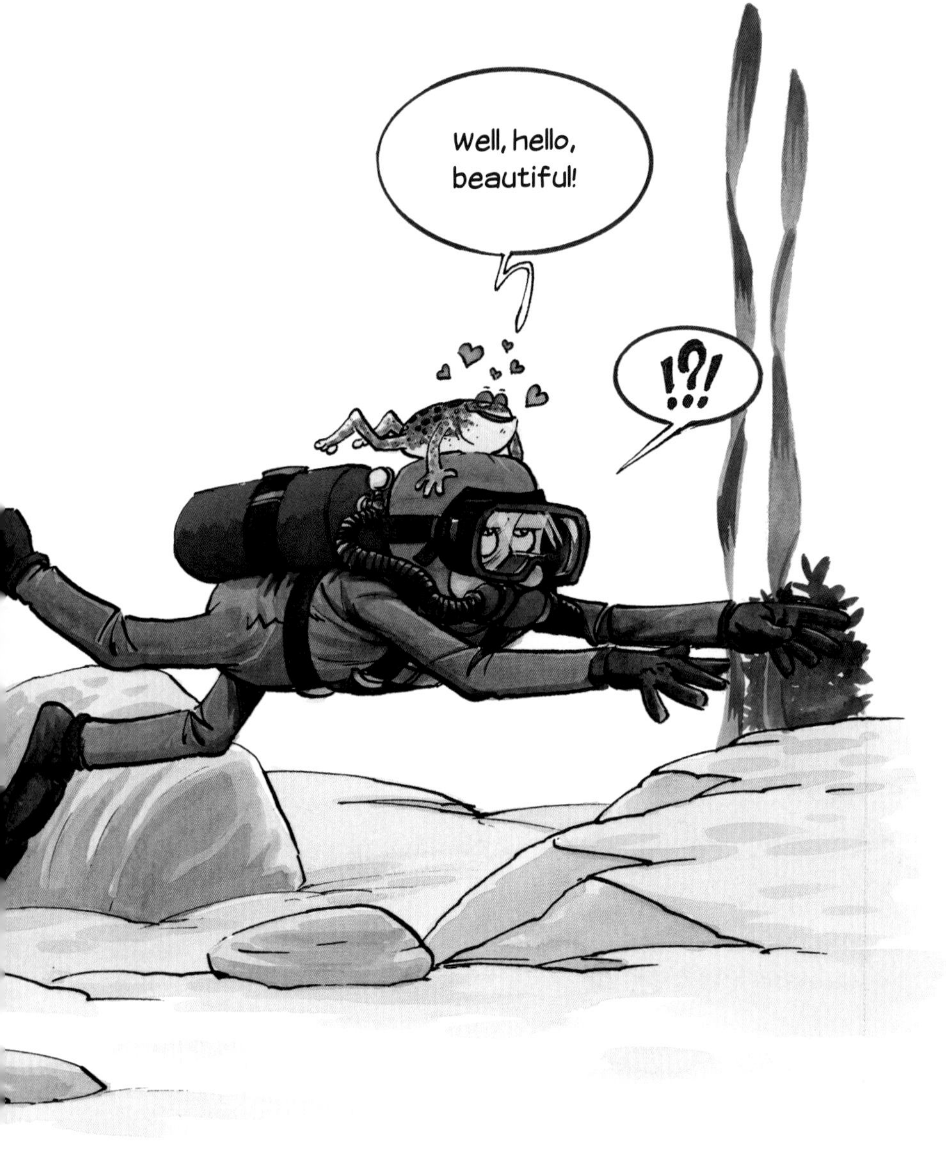
Well, hello, beautiful!
!?!

Sometimes, a male toad will accidentally try to mate with another male. However, a disapproving croak will quickly discourage him.

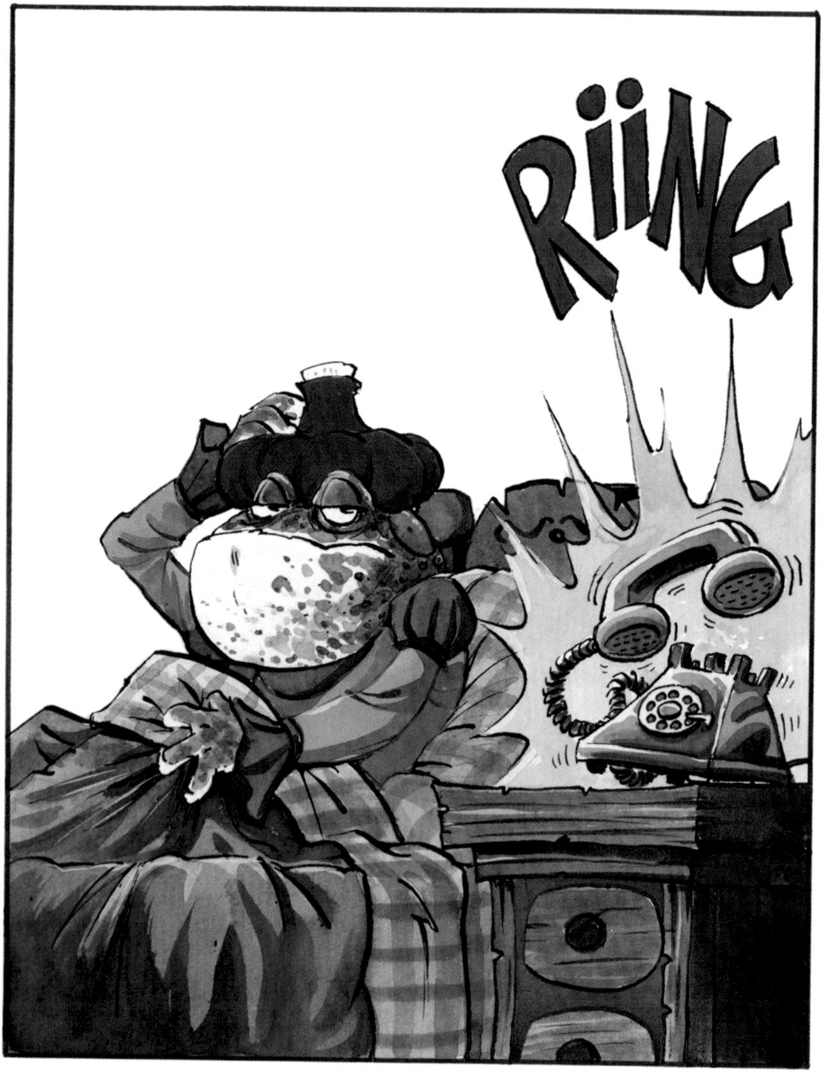
RIING

It's rare that a male will try to mate with a female that has already laid eggs.

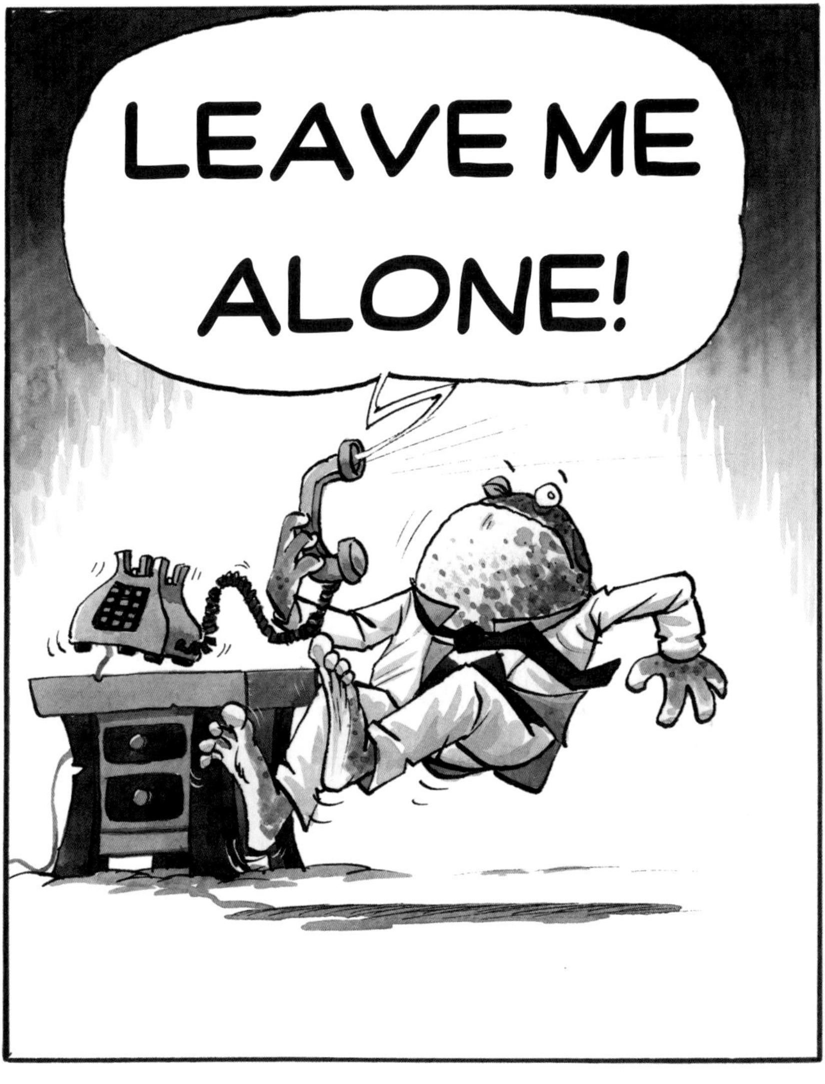
LEAVE ME ALONE!

When this does occur, the female produces a cry, letting him know that she has no more eggs to lay. This is enough to get the male to back off.

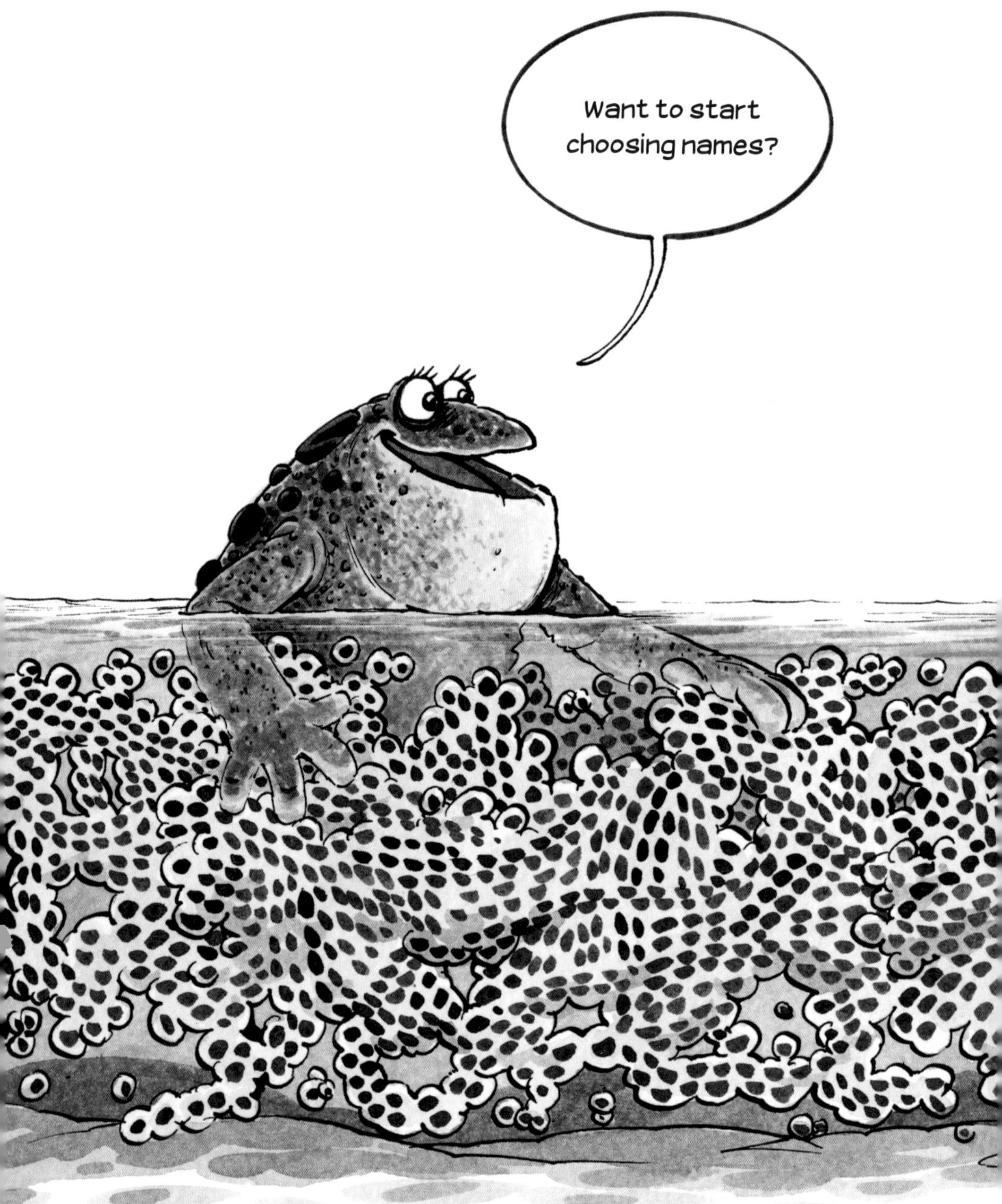
Want to start choosing names?

Females lay many thousands of eggs per season. The American toad, for example, can lay up to 25,000 eggs per mating season, and the marine toad can lay up to 30,000.

After the mating season, toads become silent and retreat back into isolation.

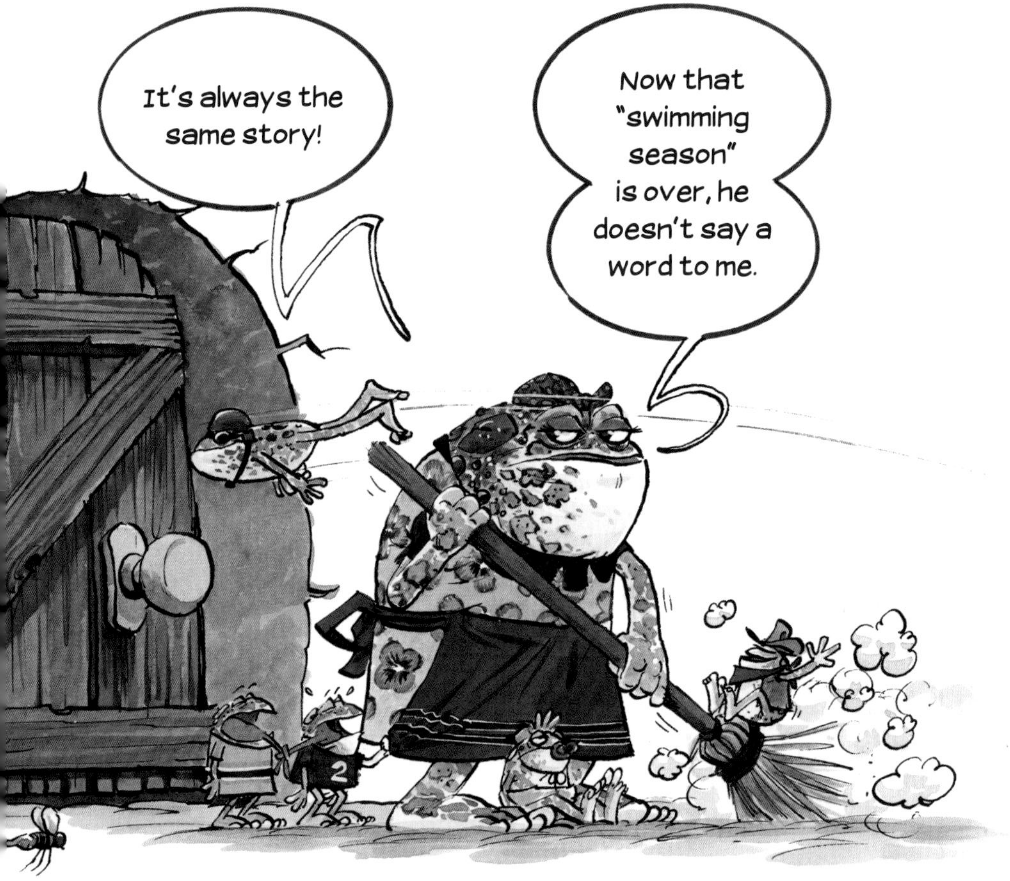
It's always the same story!
Now that "swimming season" is over, he doesn't say a word to me.

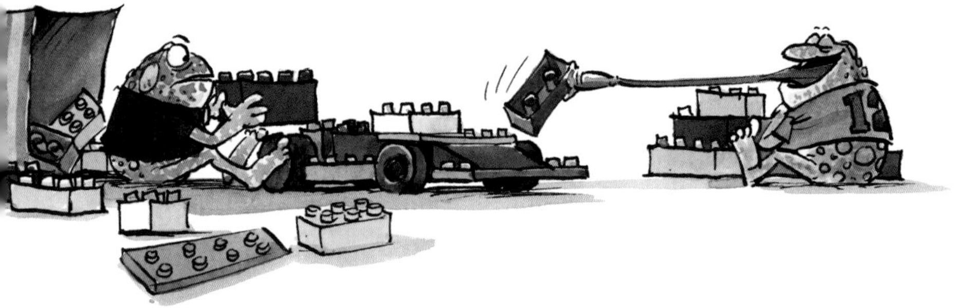

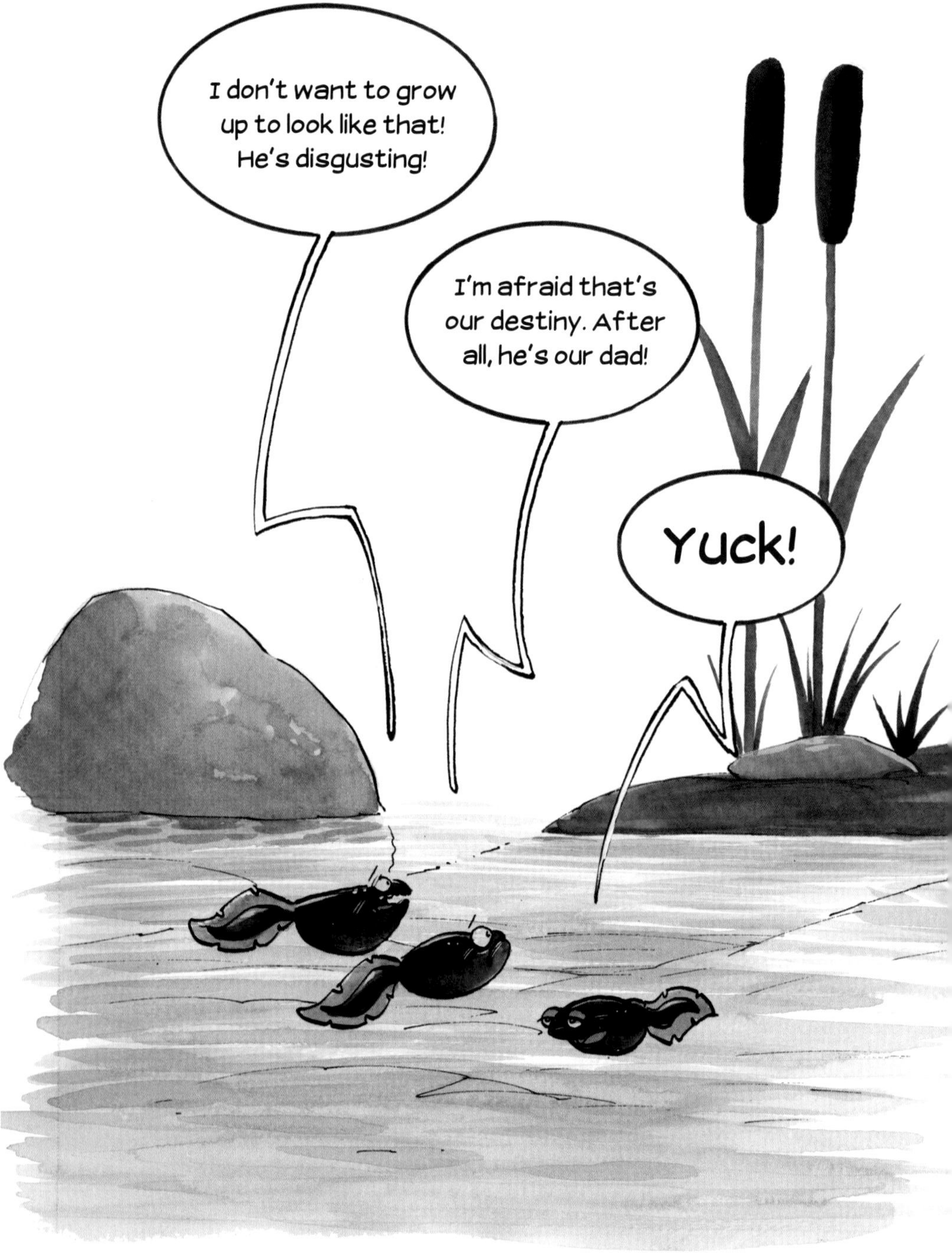
I don't want to grow up to look like that! He's disgusting!
I'm afraid that's our destiny. After all, he's our dad!
Yuck!

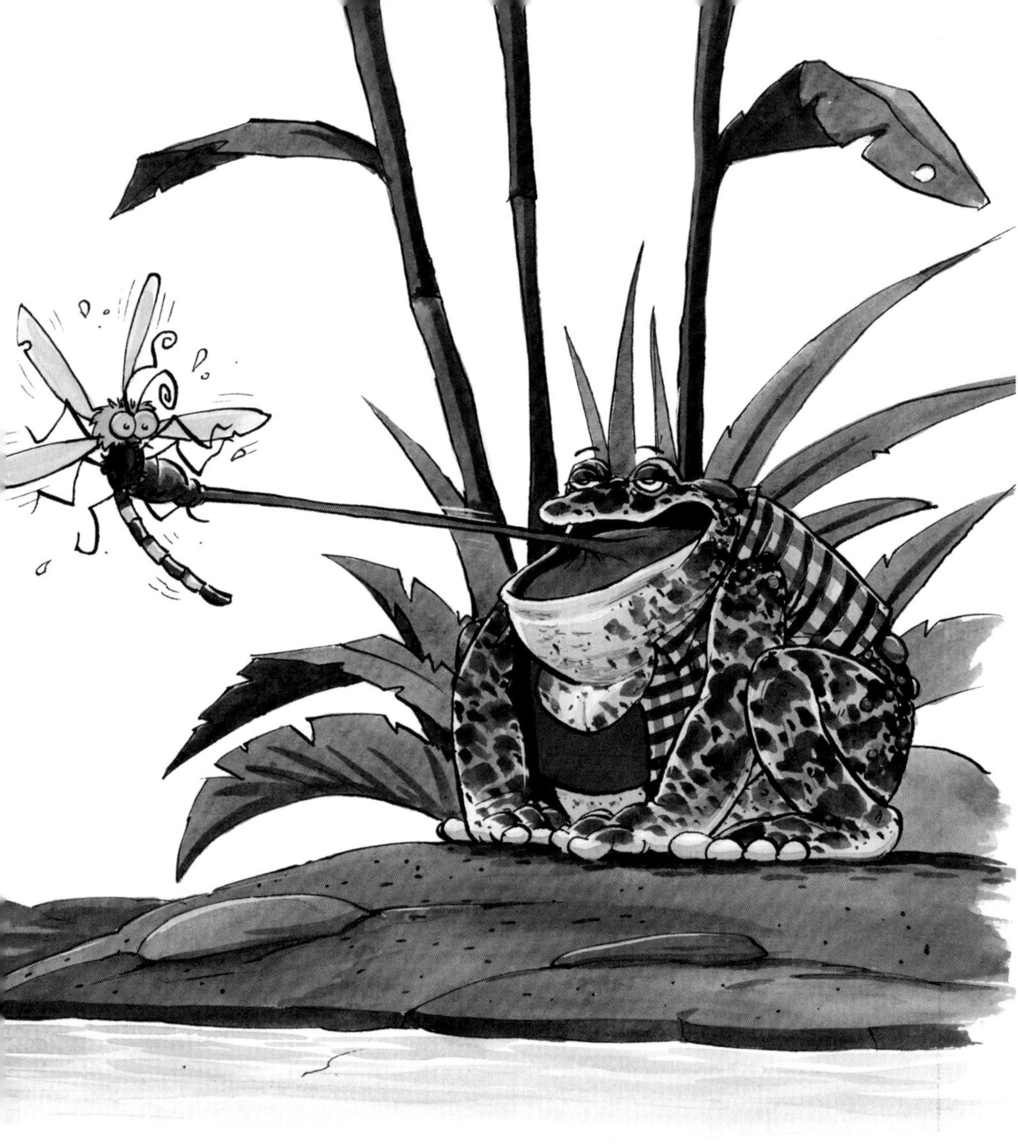

After 2-14 days, a tadpole will hatch from the egg. Unlike its parents, the tadpole breathes under water through **gills**. It also has teeth and a long tail, and eats plants.

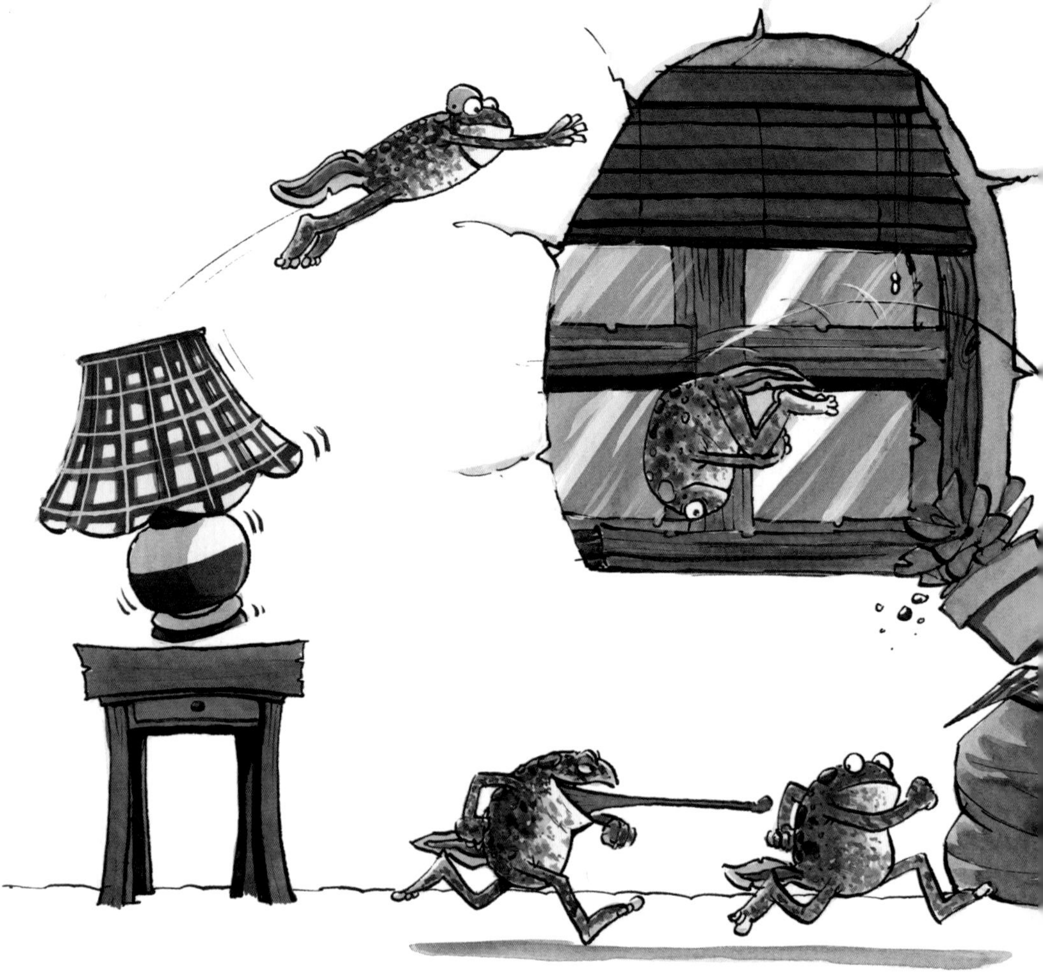

The tadpole loses its tail, gills and teeth, but grows four legs.

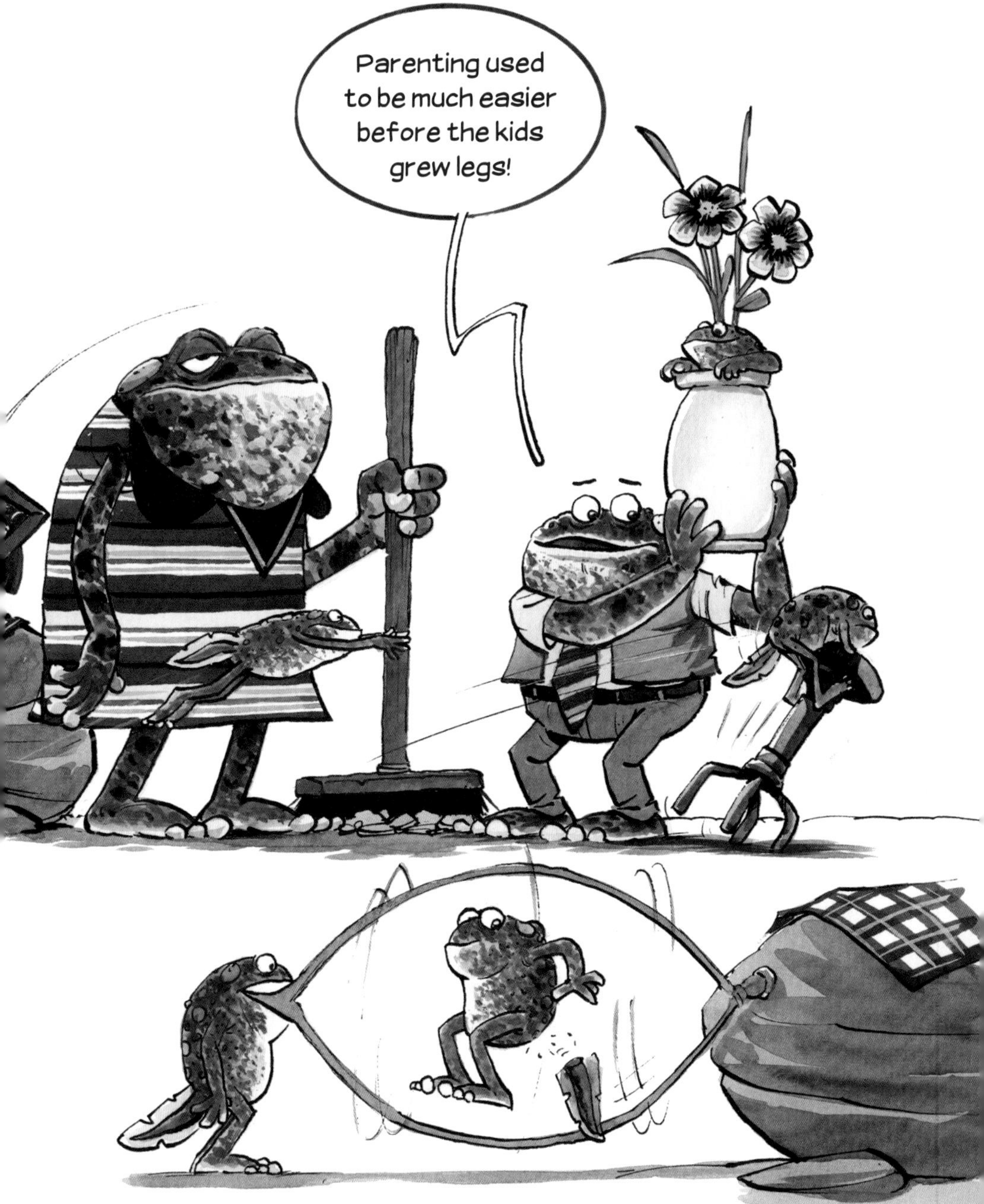
Parenting used
to be much easier
before the kids
grew legs!

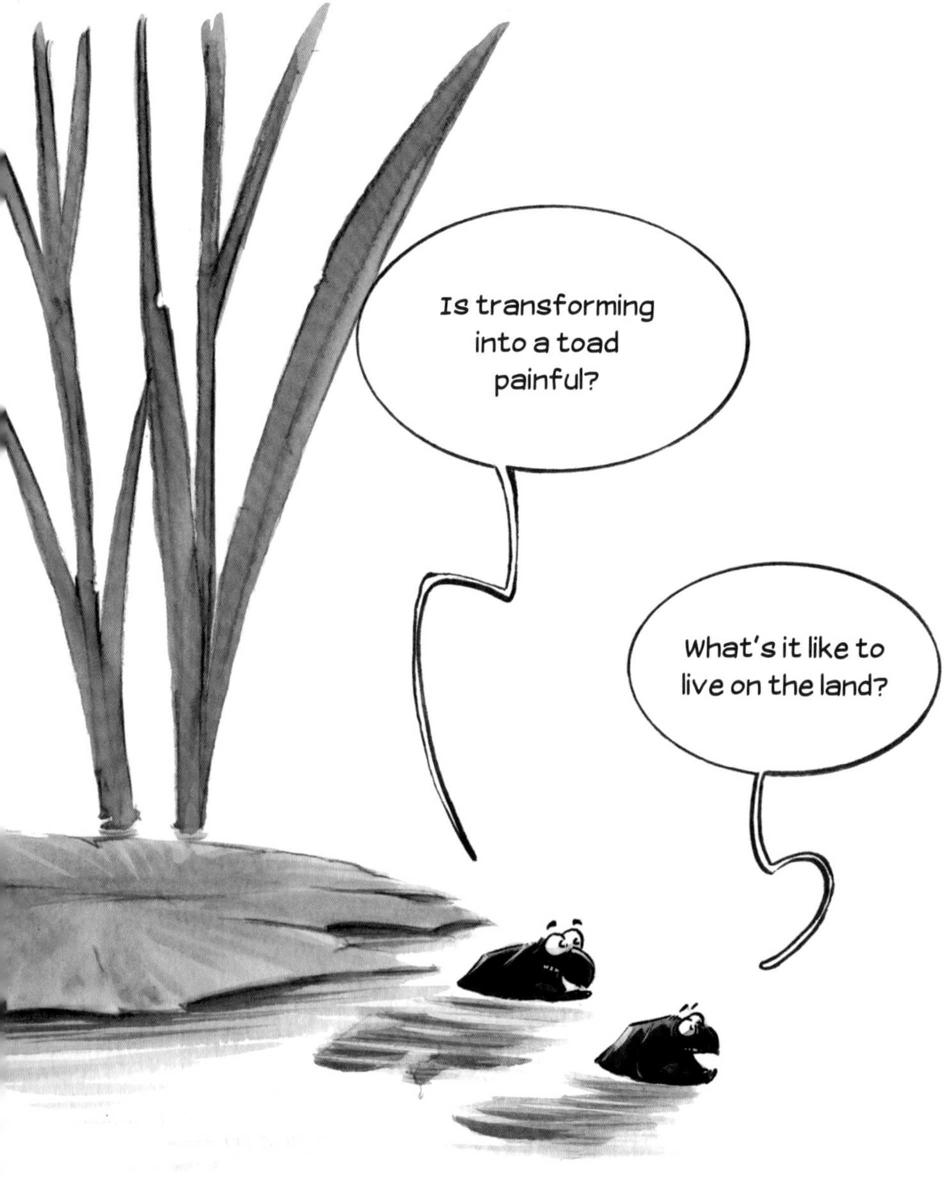
Is transforming into a toad painful?
What's it like to live on the land?

Only once the tadpole transforms into a small toad does it begin to live on land. It continues to grow throughout its entire lifetime.

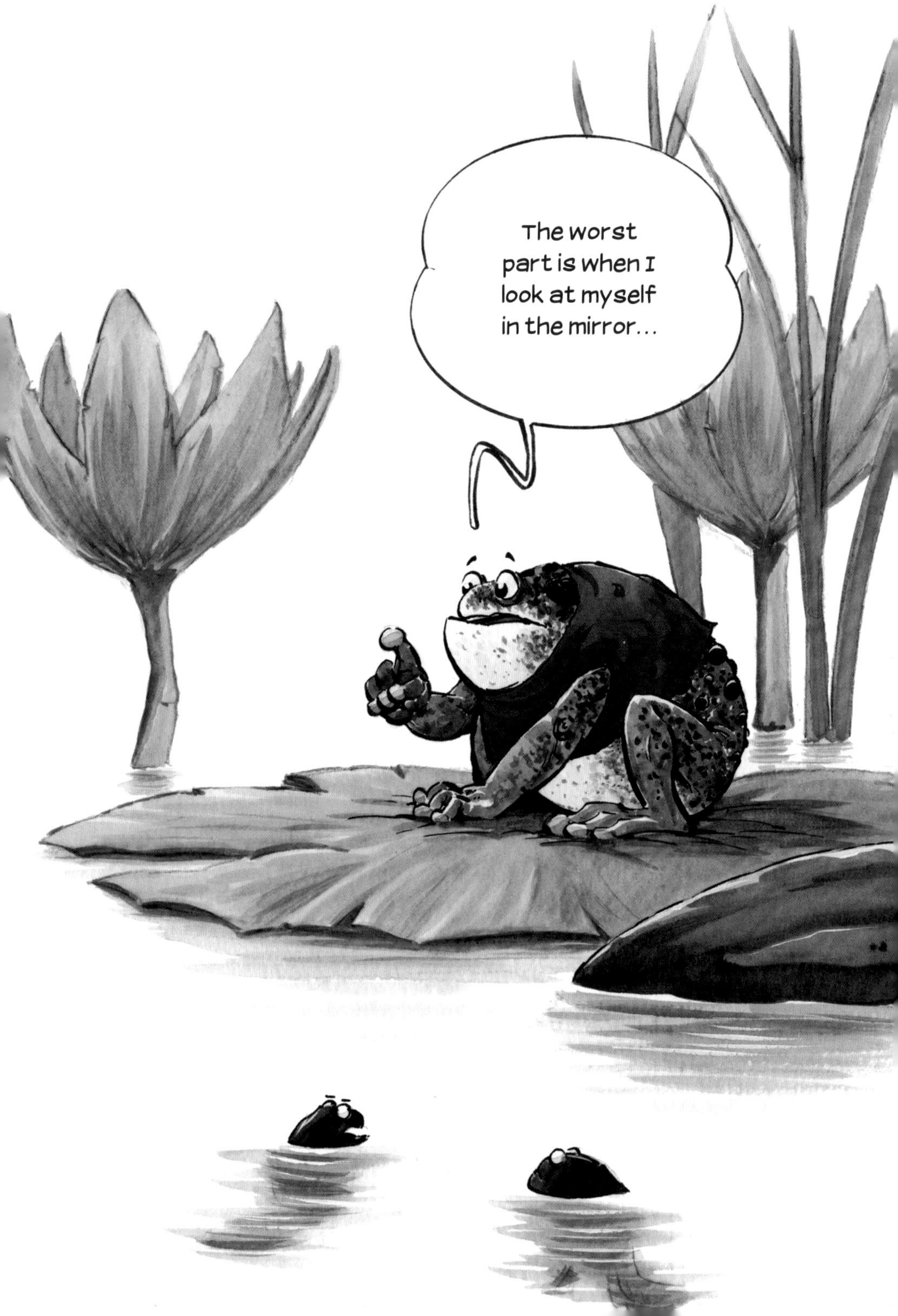
The worst part is when I look at myself in the mirror...

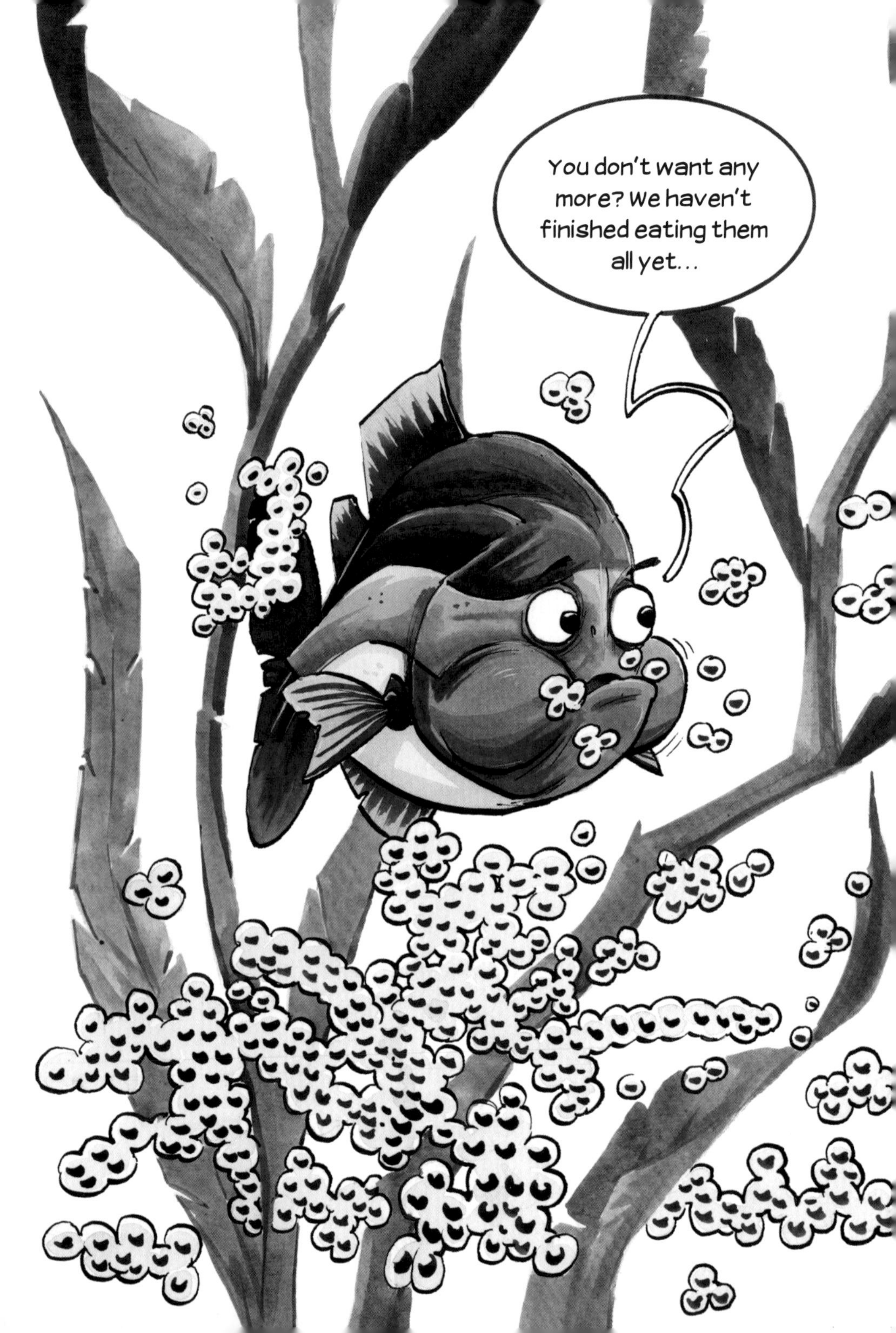
You don't want any more? We haven't finished eating them all yet...

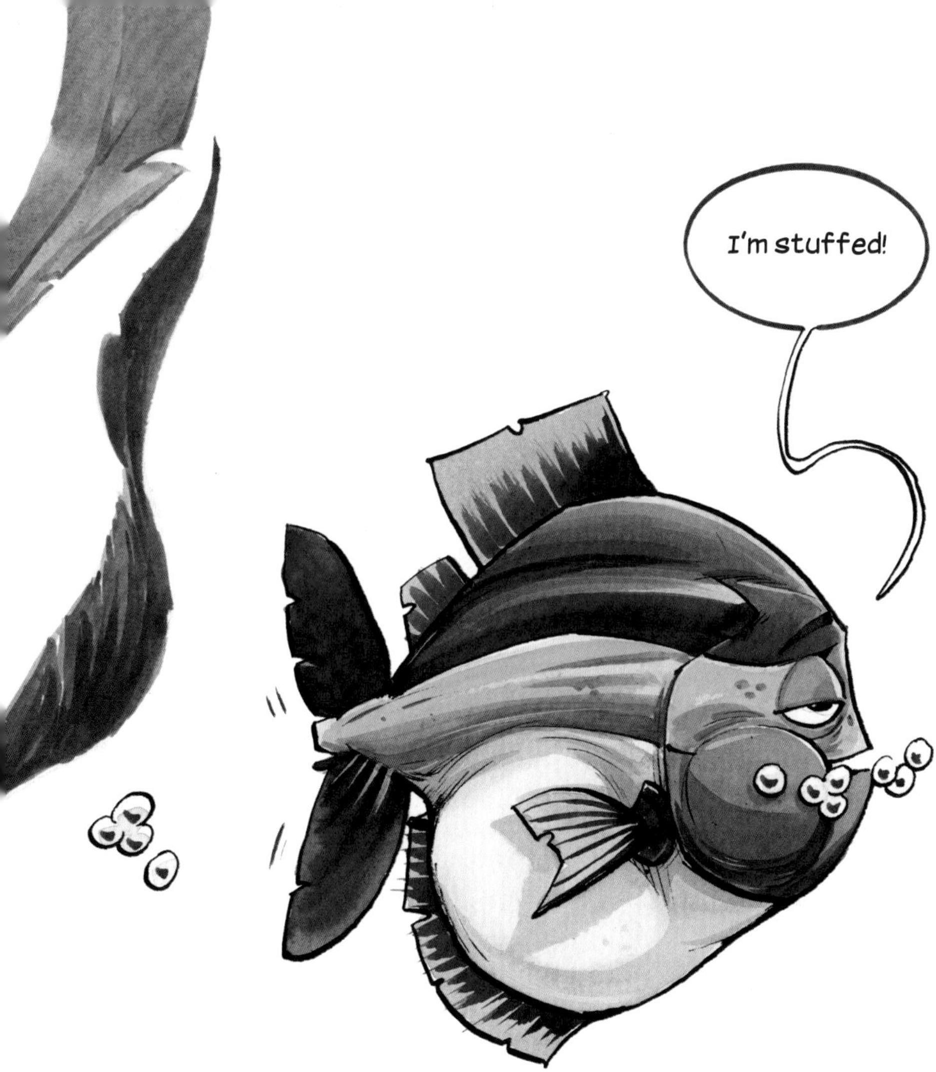
I'm stuffed!

Many toad eggs and tadpoles are eaten by fish. Toad species are able to survive mostly because the female toad is able to lay so many eggs all at once.

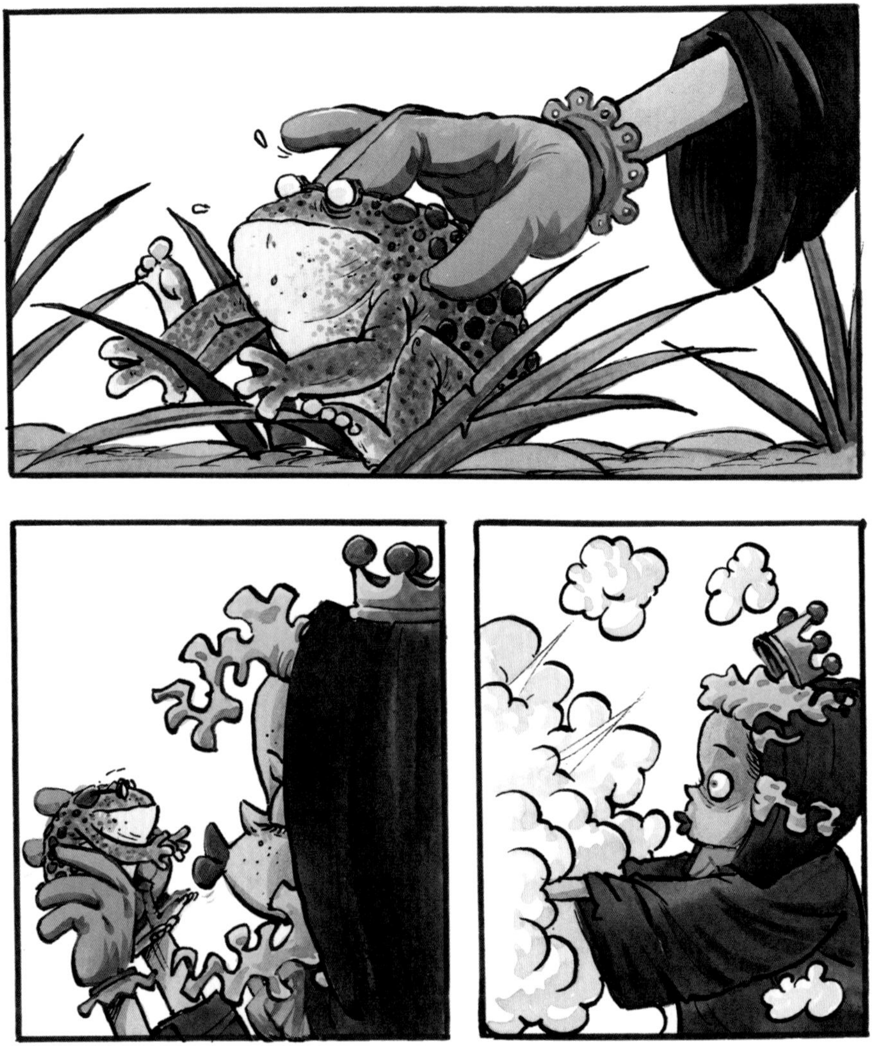

In the wild, some adult toads have lived for up to 17 years.

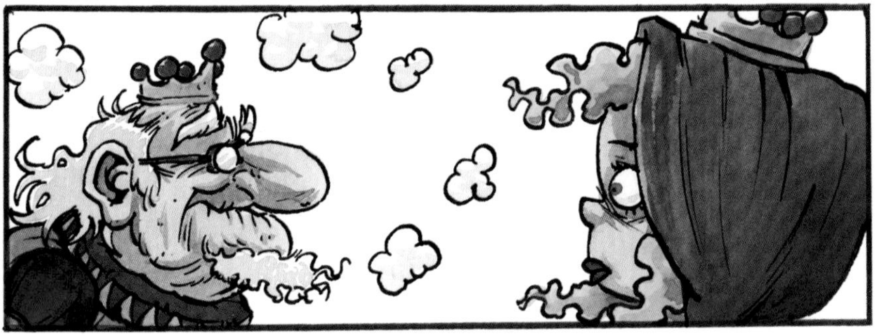

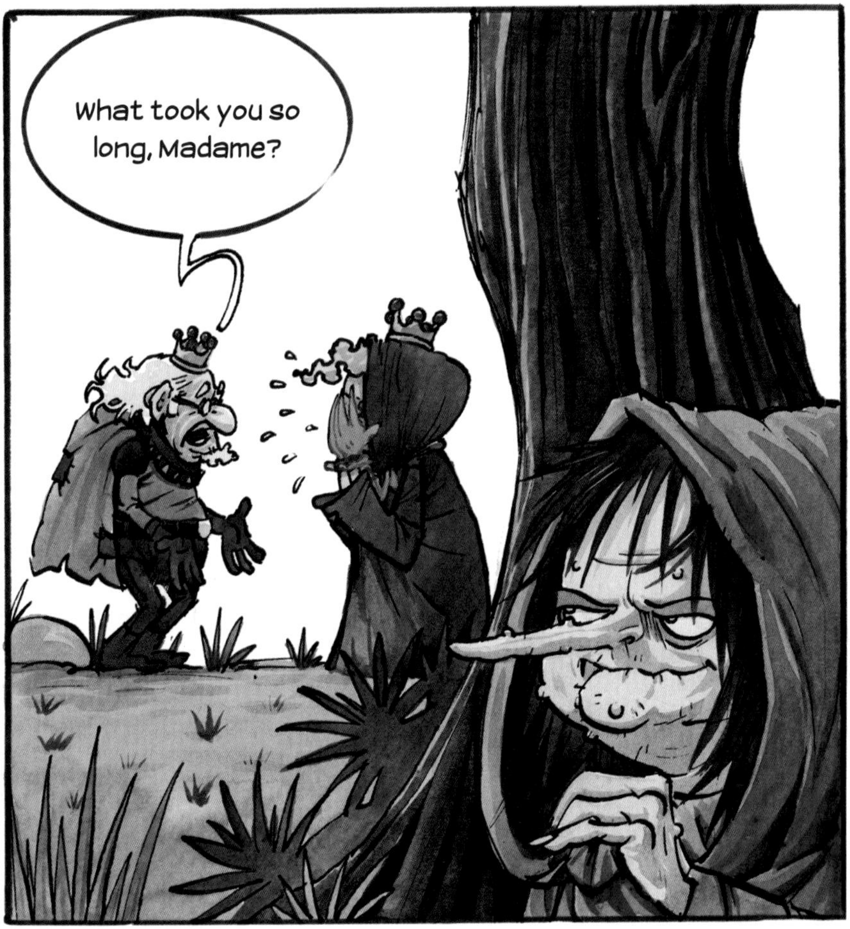
What took you so long, Madame?

Glossary

Amphibian a cold-blooded vertebrate, such as a frog, newt or salamander

Gills respiratory organs that allow certain organisms to breathe underwater

Nocturnal being active at night

Predator a hunter that kills prey for food

Prey an organism hunted and killed by another for food

Species a classification for a group of organisms with common characteristics

Terrestrial living on land, as opposed to living in the water

Torpor a state of dormant inactivity

Index

Other *Do You Know?* titles

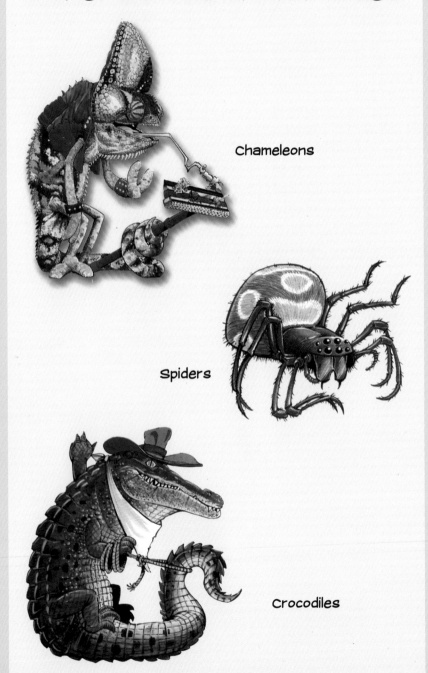

Chameleons

Spiders

Crocodiles